DROPS OF REMEMBRANCE

Second Edition

DROPS OF REMEMBRANCE

Second Edition

Juan M. Bracete

Library of Congress Control Number: 2013917492
ISBN: Hardcover   978-1-4931-0623-3
                Softcover   978-1-4931-0622-6
                Ebook   978-1-4931-0624-0

This book was printed in the United States of America.

Rev. date: 10/02/2013

To order additional copies of this book, contact:
Xlibris LLC
1-888-795-4274
www.Xlibris.com
Orders@Xlibris.com
141694

Contents

Dedication

To the Foreign Service National Employees (FSNs) at the Consular Section of the American Embassy in Caracas, Venezuela from June 1993 to June 1995 and the FSNs at the Consular Section of theAmerican Embassy in San Salvador, El Salvador from August 1995 to August 1997 without whose loyal dedication to the tasks entrusted to us the accomplishments that justified my sojourn as a Unied States Foreign Service Officer would not have been possible

A special note of gratitude is due to R. Mark Frey, Esquire of St. Paul, Minnesota without whose thoughtful and constructive review of the first edition in the April 2013 issue of *The Federal Lawyer* I would not have revisited the manuscript.

Introduction

When I joined the Foreign Service of the United States in January of 1993, little did I suspect that it would change my perception of the world in a very profound and lasting way. By the time I joined the United States Foreign Service, I had been attorney for over sixteen years, includinng five years in a medium sized firm in Puerto Rico and over four years a sole practitioner in Miami and I had been even a judge for over four years (albeit an administrative law judge with the title of immigration judge). All these work experiences gave me opportunities to experience life and life's problems in a very immediate and intense manner. Although I had had a varied and intense experience in personal and professional matters up to that time, I must be grateful for that unique opportunity offered by the Foreign Service to experience life with all its daily complications and challenges outside the United States in a non-touristic setting.

Why the Foreign Service

Many things make us tick, not all of them rational or even acknowledged by us in a conscious manner. I guess the allure of the Foreign Service had something to do with my upbringring. I was born and raised in an island, Puerto Rico. People who live in islands, like people who live in valleys surrounded by steep mountains, are fascinated by the world outside their immediate environment since it is so difficult to be out there.

I was raised in the household of my grandparents, a place where I had few choices for entertainment, other than the vast and carefully selected library accumulated by my grandfather throughout his very long and productive life. And I simply read and read of all the wonders far away from my home in the mountain, from where I could see the western shores of my small Caribbean island. And what I read simply whetted my appetite to experience that varied world outside a small tropical island where the overwhelming majority of the community was concerned with very insular interests.

Now, simply reading about the world was not the only way I found out about the big and to me marvelous world out there. My grandfather was keenly aware of his French regional heritage, Corsican to be precise. Perusing through his accumulated correspondence after his death, I realized that he really was a man of two worlds, one in this hemisphere and age and another one far away in a nebulous not now.

My grandparents took on the role of parents for me. My father married my mother and, after a couple of months of cohabitation, he was sent to the Korean Peninsula to participate in what was euphemistically called at the time the Korean Police Action. My mother returned to my grandparents' home awaiting his return from Korea.

My father returned from Korea with what would be called today posttraumatic stress disorder. My grandparents and my mother agreed that I should remain in the custody of my grandparents. Thereafter, there was never any serious attempt to reunite me with my parents. After my parents eventual divorce, there was no serious attempt to reunite me with either of my parents.

Growing up with elderly parents makes one more mature. First, elderly parents are more deliberate in what they do and children tend to imitate what surrounds them. Second, elderly parents tend to be less spontaneous and more thoughtful; again, children acquire traits through daily osmosis. I then grew up with rather less spontaneity than my cohorts, a more deliberate way of going about things and thinking before acting.

Like all children, I was expected to keep my room tidy. Since my grandparents had too many commitments, regular household chores were not done by them and they were not expected of me.

My grandparents tried their best to be loving parents. My grandfather had long working hours, but he did make an effort to be available every evening for some quality time with me before retiring. His way of showing interest and warmth was perhaps unorthodox; he kept a conversation going with me by asking me questions about people and places in the news. I was very much aware who was President of the United States, Governor of Puerto Rico, Mayor of Mayaguez, Mayor of San Juan, Pope, President of France and Queen of Great Britain, not to mention the presidents and prime minister of the neighboring Caribbean islands (the ones that had independence at the time; we are talking about the late 50's and early 60's).

On my own, I was very much aware of the Iron Curtain. I remember distinctly an incident when I was in the ninth grade where I caused a ruckus in my classroom by accusing the United States government of betraying the Hungarians who revolted against Soviet rule in 1956; I was then 14 years of age.[1]

If there is one other thing that I remember distinctly about my childhood was the Sunday routine. Although both my grandparents were Catholic, my grandmother was not a churchgoer. The one that did not miss mass was my grandfather. He always took me with him to Sunday mass.

Sunday was his one day of the week to visit relatives. We would alternate which relatives to visit after mass. The relatives we visited were all on his side of the family. The conversations usually revolved around family history, of which everyone was very much aware of.

My grandfather's father was an immigrant from Corsica who arrived in Puerto Rico while Puerto Rico was still part of Spanish America. My great grandfather was the third brother of the same last name that arrived in Puerto Rico directly from Corsica. He and his brothers were very united and it appears that the tradition of close family ties and constant interaction

---

[1]   I was not too off the mark. In what could be interpreted an act of atonement, Congress passed the Hungarian Refugees Relief Act of July 25, 1958, P.L. 85-559, to allow persons who had fled Hungary after the Soviet repression legal status in the United States without regard to a number of formalities.

dated from the time they all were reunited in Puerto Rico in the nineteenth century. My grandfather's weekly meetings with his relatives was simply a follow through on that family tradition.

My grandfather had a constant stream of visitors from Europe, most of which spoke from passable to very good Spanish since they had all at some point in time resided in Puerto Rico. Since I was by then the only person other than my grandparents in their household, and I was fairly well behaved for my age, I had an opportunity to be close to the grown ups conversations—and I loved it. A lot of things were happening in the 1950's.

I was fascinated by the tales of travel in the Atlantic Ocean to get to Puerto Rico from Europe. At that time, there were regular transatlantic steamships making the France/Spain round trip to Puerto Rico. I was in awe of the issues of foreign exchange, exchange controls, political turmoil, exotic foods and historic sights. Most of all, I was attracted to the contact with people who were sophisticated, very debonaire and who were, in an undefinable way, much more in rapport with my grandparents and, by extension, myself than our neighbors. Although my grandparents had cordial relations with their neighbors, they seemed to me to light up like Christmas trees when their European friends came to visit us.

I first went to Europe when I was only ten years of age. I went with my grandparents in a steamship, the Antilles, belonging to a French company, the Compagnie Générale Transatlantique, from San Juan, Puerto Rico to Le Havre, France. The official language of the ship was French, but Spanish was understood by all personnel in contact with the passengers. Since bilingualism was not something common in those days in Puerto Rico, I was awed by all in the ship.

By pure coincidence, on the way to Europe the then Governor of Puerto Rico, Luis Muñoz Marin, traveled with us. Since my grandfather knew him personally, on more than one occasion we had dinner together on board the ship. The Governor obviously did not object to my presence and my grandparents thought it natural that I would join them for dinner. Sitting down to dinner with the Governor of the island at my age was for me like walking on clouds.

As anyone can imagine, I was simply in awe of all that is beautiful in the Old Continent. I spent almost two months in that trip crisscrossing Europe from the Atlantic to the Adriatic, from the English Channel to the Mediterranean by all means of transportation. Naturally, most of the traveling was done in touristic buses, but occasionally we used trains (for the first time in my life) and steamboats to cross from the European mainland to the island of Corsica and back to the continent.

The experience of moving in different modes of transportation was something entirely new to me. By the time I was growing up in Puerto Rico, the railroad had ceased operations and travel by sea to and from points in the island was never a scheduled commercial option. The only regular mode of transportation in Puerto Rico was the automobile and for those in a big hurry, travel by DC-3s to and from the three major cities in the island.

Since I had used a lot of my time precociously reading all I could at my grandfather's library, I was not entirely in the dark when I was taken to museums and other cultural sites. I can still recollect the sensation of awe at the sight of the Laoocon and His Sons sculpture and the amethyst studded bible in the Vatican Museum. Years later I returned to the Vatican Museum and I looked up that singular bible, and it was still there. Somehow seeing it again was confirmation that my trip during my childhood had not been a dream.

Since this was the world my grandfather inhabited so comfortably, and it was so different from the daily (boring for me) routine in a small Caribbean island, I yearned to be closely intertwined in that world that my grandfather was so at home in. The mustard seed had been planted. The desire to achieve, grow up and rush into the world outside the balmy Caribbean was overpowering. That mustard seed was exploding within me.

Furthermore, government was not something entirely alien to our household. My grandfather was named the French Consular Agent for my hometown, Mayaguez, when I was nine years of age. Consequently, official stamps, official correspondence and interaction with a myriad of government functionaries was something that I saw on a regular basis, given my very intense relationship with my grandfather; and he did not mind my curiosity at his comings and goings.

All the free time I had as a child I used reading in our library or being around my grandfather's office. My grandfather's office was a wonderland for me, being the venue of a constant stream of persons from all walks of life, the busy buzz of business comings and goings and my occasional trip outside the office to accompany messengers on errands. Now that I think about it, how did I ever get around to do my homework?

But I must be frank. I was a lousy student until the ninth grade. I guess I was bored by school since I had so much to keep me interested outside school and homework. Ninth grade was an important milestone in my school experience. A very perceptive teacher saw through me and managed to convince me that although boring, I had to do a good job at school if I really wanted to enter the world of my grandfather when I grew up. From then on, I became a very good high school student.

My grandparents were concerned by the fact that I had few friends and that I was growing up rather a recluse. They decided that I needed more interaction with people my age. They sent me to a boarding school. Although possibly a very wise move on their part, I did not think so at the time and I was rather resentful. However, I endured my time in the boarding school as best as I could and did not attempt to flee the place like some other of my classmates had done.

However, my high school diploma was not from the boarding school. The last semester of my high school was spent in an experimental public school in my home town for children with special aptitudes. My special aptitude was in mathematics. I did not pursue that field after graduating from high school.

Transitioning from high school to college was more haphazard than it should have been. The reason was that I finished high school one year ahead of schedule. With the transition to the experimental high school I became a student without a homeroom. It felt uncomfortable. I, therefore, decided to graduate from high school ahead of schedule and I did manage to do so in the summer by sitting for home study examinations for some of the required classes in the curriculum to obtain the high school diploma.

Now, no college applications had been made. Thankfully, the Mayaguez Campus of the University of Puerto Rico was headed by a very kind man and he obviated the formalities for my admission to the campus in light of my exceptionally good grades in high school. I would like to think that he also appreciated my resourcefulness in getting out of high school on my own one year ahead of schedule. I entered the Mayaguez Campus of the University of Puerto Rico before my seventeenth birthday.

My grandfather was not a bystander in all of this. Although he expected me to do the groundwork, he backed my efforts by facilitating the logistics of going places and securing information to achieve my goal of entering college ahead of schedule. That is one think my grandfather taught me, self-reliance.

I rushed through high school and I rushed through college. I did my high school diploma in three years. I did my bachelor's degree in three years. I studied the summers and I overloaded on course work during the regular semesters. I just could not hold still.

That eagerness to be out was, however, not without cost. By rushing through high school and college and not keeping in step with my cohorts, I lost a reference group without gaining another one. That instilled in me the need for self reliance without the possibility of a fall back. I always felt very lonely since along the way I lost my grandmother, who was like a mother to me, and my grandfather, being busy remaking his life, lost some interest in me.

Since I had been attending mostly private schools before entering the University of Puerto Rico, the public university, I had an advantage over most of my classmates. Private schools in Puerto Rico at that time were certainly much more competitive than public schools. Also, since my university classmates did not seem as motivated as I was, I found little in common with them and I kept mostly to myself during my freshman year. Before I had finished the first semester at the Mayaguez campus of the University of

Puerto Rico, I knew, with all the certainly in the world, that I would make my life abroad.

Although a good university in terms of technical matters, the Mayaguez Campus of the University of Puerto Rico left much to be desired in the liberal arts and anything that was not pure or applied science. At that time, the Mayaguez Campus of the University of Puerto Rico was the place to train in engineering and agricultural sciences. One had the feeling that all other subjets were mere afterthoughts or worse. I finished my first semester with excellent grades and I began my quest for the holy grail of studying off the island.

I was not much encouraged in my itch to study abroad by the person who counted the most in this, my grandfather. So I had to do it all, and I really mean all, by myself to find out about possible universities outside of Puerto Rico and how to go about gaining admission with no encouragement other than my inner self. I looked up possible universities in the United States and I wrote to them for the application packages. You can well imagine what the response was from almost all the institutions I made contact with. Somehow my dedication to excellence and my stubborn perseverance did not shine through in my initial contacts with the various stateside admissions offices.

But destiny will not be sidetracked, especially for those that just keep at it. I found an ally in a very good friend of my grandfather who had studied at Georgetown University and who kept very good relations with the then powers that be at that institution. He guided me to the right person at Georgetown (a kind and at that time elderly Jesuit priest) and I was able to squeak into that university as a transfer student straight into the sophomore year. With admission letter in hand, I approached my grandfather: I simply presented him with a *fait accompli* and I managed to get his reluctant approval, undoubtedly because he knew that otherwise I would be a very uncooperative live-in grandson from then on.

Being admitted as a transfer student and given credit for courses taken at the University of Puerto Rico were essential for my successful completion of my bachelor's degree outside of Puerto Rico. This was because my grandfather made it clear that he had budgeted a certain amount for the college education of each of his grandchildren (there were twenty-three of us at that time) and that I was going to receive no more and no less than what he had budgeted for each. So, I knew I was embarking on a trip filled with not only an academic challenge but also an economic one. However, the full extent of the economic challenge was not perceived by me evident until later.

I remember very well registration day at Georgetown that fall of 1969. I walked into the registrar's office and in my less than fluent English I navigated the process of selecting and registering into my courses for the first semester. The assistant registrar that took care of me was very congratulatory of my performance in accomplishing everything so well with my obvious lingusitic handicap. But happiness was short lived.

My first week of classes was a challenge. Although I could read and comprehend very well written English, understanding spoken English at the University level complexity was a challenge. But that was secondary to my trepidation at the prospect of what I was supposed to do to successfully complete my course work. The Puerto Rico educational system up to that point in my studies had not required me to do independent research and present the research in written format with due regard to sources, citations and logical presentation. The term "term paper" was up to then unknown to me.

Friday of that first week came and I got despondent. I could not bring myself to believe that I could actually do it. My reaction was to call my mother and tell her that I could not do it and that I wanted to go back to Puerto Rico. She, poor soul, told me not to worry and just hop on the first available plane back to Puerto Rico.

After I hung up the telephone, I marshaled the facts. First, the school fees had been paid and there would be no refund. Second, the university school year began in Puerto Rico earlier than in the Mainland United States and there was no way I could register that late to complete the semester at the University of Puerto Rico (I had not formally quitted the University of Puerto Rico). Third, there was the fact that my grandfather would remind me what his position was on studying off island right from the beginning.

So, after thinking this through, I decided that I had no immediate need to return to Puerto Rico then and there and that I might as well give it a try and see what happened. Sunday evening I called my mother and told her that I was sticking through the semester.

Well, my English comprehension improved considerably after a couple of weeks. Second, I bought a term paper guide (that I still have) and decided to self-teach myself on how to do a term paper. And I did very well. I finished my first semester at Georgetown University in the Dean's List.

The self confidence that came from that successful first semester carried me through the various hoops I had to go through to actually finish my bachelor's degree at Georgetown. The economic issue came into better focus after I tallied the expenses incurred in that first semester at Georgetown. I only had money through one semester short of Georgetown studies. I knew that my grandfather meant what he said about footing the bill only as he would foot the bill of any other of his grandchildren.

So, I overbooked myself with course work during the next semester and kept doing so until I graduated. But that would not be enough. I had to study the summer.

Where to study during the summer was an issue. I could not study in the Washington area due to the economics. I had to study in Puerto Rico where

I would not have to pay lodging and where credit courses were cheaper than in the Washington area.

What to study during the summer was also an issue. It would be impossible to study in Puerto Rico courses that would fit into my core curriculum at Georgetown. What was left was the required courses in Catholic dogma required for Catholic students, two one-semester courses. But that would not be enough to complete the required number of courses for graduation. So, I added two sessions of philosophy to my summer load at the Catholic University of Puerto Rico. During the summer of 1970, I did four one-semester courses. The Dean of the School of Business Administration at Georgetown University was very understanding. He approved my taking the summer courses in Puerto Rico and gave me full credit for the four courses as if I had taken them at Georgetown.

I was within sight of my goal. And May 1971 arrived and I graduated first in my class of one hundred fourteen students. Another break I got to speed up my degree was the waiver by Georgetown University of the world history requirement. This was done on the basis of my 99th percentile ranking in the world history SAT elective examination. Extensive and voracious reading in my grandfather's library during my childhood and adolescence wrought a very tangible real life benefit.

Then I returned to Puerto Rico when I could not find employment in the Washington, D.C. area (the only area in the United States that I knew). My return to Puerto Rico after the university experience at Georgetown University was not a happy occasion; I felt like a failure and the return a defeat. I immediately began to work in Puerto Rico in banking as a junior credit officer at the largest and oldest savings and loan association in the island. I was able to get that job almost immediately after I returned to Puerto Rico thanks to the same friend who got me the opportunity to be considered as a transfer student at Georgetown University.

My stint at the savings and loan association was rather short since I was offered about six months later employment at another banking institution with a very generous salary increase. I had a lot of responsibility for a person in his early twenties. I thrived on the opportunity to excel. Consequently, I was regularly promoted, becoming a junior credit officer in the division of the bank in charge of financing small and medium sized businesses. Even with such accomplishments, I felt so bored that I began to study law in the evenings. Why I studied law and not something else begins with a very quaint anecdote.

I can state with absolute certainty the day I knew I was going to evenually be an attorney. The certainty came from the realization on that particular day in 1968 that I was good at advocating. The setting was my classroom at the public school I spent my last semester of high school.

One of the class assignments was reading a then very popular Venezuelan novel entitled Doña Bárbara by Romulo Gallegos. This novel has been described as the most widely known Latin American novel. The teacher asked the class if we wanted to make a class project of the novel. I ventured if we could do as a project putting Doña Bárbara on trial for the murder she committed in the novel. The teacher liked the idea and we set about to assign roles for the trial.

I volunteered to take the role of defense attorney. My classmates gladly let me have the role since it was evident Doña Bárbara had committed the murder of the person she was going to be placed on trial for.

Well, I took my role very seriously. At that time, Perry Mason was a very popular television series. And I was a steadfast fan of the show. And I followed the script of the television show. I followed it so well that I had the jury (the largest part of the class), come out with a verdict of not guilty.

I was congratulated by all on my performance (which was more theatrical than I would like to admit) as defense attorney. And I knew then and there that some day I would be an attorney by profession.

Diplomacy was not then in my field of vision. But now that I think about it, diplomacy is really advocating the interests of the sending state before authorities of other states and international organizations.

But nothing comes easy in life. After two years of attending evening law school, I was faced with a difficult choice by the bank I was working for during the day. Management wanted me to go to a training course abroad (Mexico), lasting six months. This meant interrupting my law studies (no distance learning at that time). To boot, the six months were right in the middle of two semester, which meant I would have to postpone my law degree for one full year.

Existential decisions sneak on you. I tried to wiggle out of going then to the training course, offering to go later, but management was adamant that it was then that I had to go. So, after a lot of soul searching, I came back to them with my resignation in hand. There were then some half hearted attempts on their part to have me backtrack, but I told them that they would never forget that I had forced their hands, and so my decision to leave banking and become a full time law student became irrevocable.

And then I became a full time student. Instead of four years (the regular evening law school track), it took me three and a half years to finish my law degree, right between the three years of day law school and the four years of night law school. The transition from evening school to day school went smoothly. However, again I was depriving myself of a reference group by not graduating with the people I began the career and graduating with people that did not know me.

Since I was then married, and I did not want to loaf around the summer before my last semester, I applied for an internship at the United States Department of Justice in Washington, D.C. I was assigned to the Tax Division to assist with two major litigation matters, one involving the allowance of depreciation of certain railroad assets with rather long useful lives and the other with who had the right to claim depreciation when property was not owned in fee simple. Of course, my role in the two matters was small, although I prefer to think not inconsequential. Eventually, both cases were settled. But I got out of the experience the research material for my first law review article.

That summer intership opened the way for my first permanent job as an attorney. I applied through the Department of Justice Honors Program right after my return from Washington to Puerto Rico to resume my law degree. Of course, my first choice was employment with the Tax Division of the Justice Department, where I thought I had made a good impression and where I felt quite at ease in the mix between law and accounting. But fate had another road for me.

My offer for employment under the Honors Program came from an entity within the Department of Justice totally unknown to me at that time: the Board of Immigration Appeals. When I received the phone call from the recruiter I could not quite know what to answer. On the one hand I certainly wanted a job in the Washington area with the Department of Justice. On the other hand, immigration law was totally alien to me (no pun intended).

My need for a job and the enthusiasm of the recruiter was a winning combination. He offered to fly down to Puerto Rico to interview me. The interview went on extremely well. He told me not to worry about the lack of knowledge of immigration matters; it was part of the indoctrination process (that was exactly the word used) to send new attorneys hired by the Board of Immigration Appeals to a graduate level immigration law course at Georgetown University taught by the then undisputed guru of immigration law, Charles Gordon. That cynched the deal; going back to school at Georgetown University from where I had secured my bachelor's degree was quite an inducement for me.

The day came for me to start work at the Board of Immigration Appeals. The supervisory staff was amiable and the coworkers were very receptive. My days at the Board were professionally fulfilling and personally gratifying. When the time came for me to depart from the Board on account of pressing family concerns that counseled my return to Puerto Rico, my decision to resign was fraught with sadness. But, as the saying goes, you have to do what you have to do.

I returned to Puerto Rico because my grandfather, who was also my foster father, became terminally ill. Since he had always shown a great deal of affection and concern for my well being, my heart would not allow me to keep away from him during his last few months on this earth. I returned to Puerto Rico to be able to see him frequently, which I did. I returned to Puerto Rico without a job. I really like to live dangerously.

But God provides for madmen, children and fools. Soon after my arrival in Puerto Rico, a childhood friend who like me had studied law in the Mainland United States informed me that the law firm at which he worked was looking for an attorney with my background, although not necessarily my experience. Since I had little to lose and much to gain, I immediately whipped up a resume (I departed Washington without even having drafted a resume), and telephoned the law firm to ask for an interview with the hiring partner. The interview was granted.

The hiring partner and I hit it off stupendously. If someone from Mars had been there, he would have taken the meeting to be a reunion of long lost friends. I made the rounds of all the partners in the law firm and, of course, went by my friend's office (it was no secret that we were friends and that I had asked for an interview on the basis of his recommendation). Of course, no hiring decision of a professional is usually made then and there and I was called in for a second interview the Friday of that same week, at 4:30 PM (if that was not a give away, I don't know what is).

The Friday came and I went in for the second interview. They were very apologetic that they could not offer me a starting salary matching what I had been earning at the Board of Immigration Appeals. But, that was not really an issue for me and I told them that I accepted. Then they told me that they were celebrating the success in a very important litigation matter and that they were all going out after work to have a couple of drinks at a very well known cocktail lounge and I was invited to join them.

Well, I learned there what a couple of drinks meant in that milieu. We sat down at a table and we were lavished with all sorts of finger food and . . . bottle after bottle of Dom Perignon. Although I did not grow up in a deprived environment, I had never drunk Dom Perignon in my life—and I liked it. I liked it so much that I almost tore down my mother's gate when I returned home in a state that could charitably be described as semi catatonic.

I worked at that law firm for almost six years. The first nine months coincided with my grandfather's terminal illness. It was for me a period of readaptation to Puerto Rico, now as an attorney. I learned the ropes of the trade and I did well. Some would say that I did extremely well since my annual salary increments and my year end bonuses placed me in the top 10 per cent of wage earners in Puerto Rico.

But my heart was not in private practice, nor in living in Puerto Rico. Soon after my grandfather passed away I began my efforts to return to government service in the mainland. It was not easy. I soon found out that saying goodbye to a government job almost always means you are out for good. But I persevered.

I had always kept very good relations with my former supervisors in Washington. It came to be that, in an effort to give more prestige and independence to immigration judges, the hiring and supervision of the immigration judge corps was transferred from the then Immigration and Naturalization Service to the newly created Executive Office for Immigration Review whose Director was at that time also the Chairman of the Board of Immigration Appeals, my former boss. And it came to pass that I was actually began work as an immigration judge in Miami almost exactly six years after my departure from the Board of Immigration Appeals.

When I applied for the immigration judge position in Miami, I had never been to Florida. I applied for the job on the basis of the work itself and not on considerations about the location. When I finally got the offer of employment, I made a specific trip to Miami to look up the place where I would be working. Now, if that is not Foreign Service attitude, I really do not know what it is.

My work in immigration law
prior to the Foreign Service

My work at the Board of Immigration Appeals was a very satisfying experience. First, I learned about a field of law that I did not even know existed prior to my job interview. Second, I had the opportunity of learning the intricacies of the field from the acknowledged master of the subject matter at the time, Charles Gordon. Third, I had the opportunity to hone my research skills by looking into novel issues not only of federal law, but of states and foreign countries.

United States immigration law is a truly complex field. In addition to the purely immigration law rules set by Congress from time to time (and which can change retroactively at the will of Congress), the administration of the immigration laws looks at the domestic law of the individual states and foreign countries to determine the validity of family relationships. So, a marriage may be a legal marriage if contracted in one jurisdiction, and will be recognized for immigration purposes, but the same marriage if contracted in another jurisdiction that considers it illegal will not be recognized for immigration purposes.

Not only marriages have to pass the local jurisdiction test, but also divorces. A divorce may be legal where obtained but if it is not recognized by the jurisdiction of the place where one of the divorced parties contracts a second marriage, then that second marriage will not be recognized for United States immigration purposes. Immigration adjudicators routinely look into these matters, to the surprise of many.

The same goes for adoptions. The immigration adjudicator will scrutinize the adoption papers to ascertain if the adoption is legal where performed and where the parties are domiciled at the time of the adoption.

This was the bread and butter of Board of Immigration Appeals work at the time I was working there. We had a continuous flow of appeals from persons denied immigration benefits because the then Immigration and

Naturalization Service would not recognize a divorce, marriage, adoption or legitimation based on the law of the domicile of the parties or of the place of celebration. At the Board of Immigration Appeals, we were forced to research individual state or foreign country law to ascertain if the initial adjudicator's call was the right one.

When the time came for me to depart the Board of Immigration Appeals, I had acquired quite an expertise in research, not only of United States law, but also how to go about doing research of foreign law.

When I was hired by the law firm in Puerto Rico after my departure from the Board of Immigration Appeals, that expertise was not necessarily the tipping issue to offer me the job. The firm in San Juan needed someone who would feel at home working in English. Two years and seven months at the Board of Immigration Appeals fulfilled that requirement.

But, I did practice immigration law at the Puerto Rico law firm. The firm had as clients a number of multinational manufacturing companies that routinely transferred executives, managers and specialized workers throughout their facilities worldwide. When they realized that I was there, work relating to the transfer to Puerto Rico of executives, managers and specialized workers that would normally be done by their headquarters outside counsel was contracted with the Puerto Rico firm.

Some cases were less than clear-cut, as is the case in a rather large number of cases. Advocacy skills still make the difference in those cases. Given my credibility as a former staff attorney at the Board of Immigration Appeals, my advocacy of a case sometimes made the difference.

And it allowed me to travel. On more than occasion I was called upon to defend the initial favorable decision when questioned at the port of entry. This involved spur of the moment travel to represent the unfortunate transferee before the immigration judge at the port of entry.

In one particular case, the issue was so groundless that I almost laughed in the face of the immigration judge. He was applying a rule that had been revoked by legislation and he was totally oblivious of the change in the law. From the port of entry I flew to Washington, DC to write my brief at the library of the Board of Immigration Appeals and I mailed the brief from that facility. Needless to say, the transferee got in.

My work as an immigration judge in Miami was at a time when the vast majority of cases coming before the Miami immigration judges involved requests for asylum from Haitians and Cubans. Unfortunately, there was the impression of bias due to the fact that Cuban, due to the Cuban Adjustment Act of 1966 (still on the books), generally got to stay and Haitian generally were ordered deported.

Haiti in the early 1980's was a source of a continuous flow of refugees seeking asylum. Most of them, unfortunately, did not qualify under the guidelines of the asylum process. Haitian, by and large, could not prove that they would be persecuted if returned to Haiti due to race, religion, nationality, membership in a particular social group or political opinion. Consequently, they were ordered deported. Those orders of deportation were generally affirmed by the Board of Immigration Appeals.

When an immigration judge denied asylum to a Cuban on the same grounds, he would appeal, just as a Haitian would. By the time the appeal came for adjudication by the Board of Immigration Appeals, the Cuban would be entitled to residence status under the Cuban Adjustment Act of 1966 and the denial of asylum would become moot. Same facts but different nationalities resulted in different results.

Many immigration judges, aware of this, would find ways to postpone Cuban deportation cases until the Cuban national could apply for residence status under the Cuban Adjustment Act of 1966. I did not do so because I wanted to handle all my cases evenly. If my decision became moot later, so be it. That irritated many people.

One Cuban attorney, whose name I will reserve, one day stated in open court that it would be better for my health if I were to depart from the Miami area. I could not believe my ears when I heard her words.

I immediately called a recess and I telephoned the Office of the Chief Immigration Judge in Washington to report the incident. I emphasized that the statement was made in open court in the presence of various attorneys.

The attorney in question was visited by agents of the Federal Bureau of Investigation. They told her that her statements were at least obstruction of justice. However, that they were going to assume that she did not realize what she had done. But they cautioned her that she should pray that nothing happened to me because if anything happened to me, they would first arrest her and then they would continue the investigation.

When I went into private practice after my stint on the bench, I actively practiced immigration law. I had clients of all nationalities. I advocated vigorously on their behalf. I won some, I lost some.

The one case that still stands in my mind as remarkable was a client from Venezuela, who came to my office asking me to help her in filing for asylum. I explained to her that I thought the likelihood of her case being taken serious by our immigration authorities was slim since Venezuela had ostensibly a working democracy (now, we are talking about the late 1980's early 1990's). However, she insisted and she paid me a retainer.

I went to work and we filled out the paper work for filing. Her story was enthralling. She was a practicing attorney in Venezuela and she had stumbled into a purely civil litigation involving the mistress of a high government official. She had been contacted by the minions of the high government official and told to drop it or else. She, believing that she was living and working in a working democracy, continued with her litigation.

One day, she went to court to file some documents in an unrelated case. She was not allowed to file the documents because she had been declared a fugitive. The clerk of the court, with malice or not, we do not know, showed her the notice that had been sent to the courts concerning her order of arrest. Well, my client just went to airport and got on the next flight to Miami. She did well because her family informed her that that evening the police went to her home to arrest her.

Upon submission of the paperwork, the procedure then was to forward a copy to the Department of State. The Department of State generally responded to these referrals with a form letter stating they have no information on the applicant. Well, that did not happen in this case. The Department of State came back with a favorable recommendation to the grant of asylum. I was surprised and I learned my lesson never to assume anything.

The attempts to join the
Foreign Service

I must begin with the fact that I applied to join the Foreign Service of the United States for the first time in the mid-1970's. I was not yet a lawyer, but I was working full time as a bank credit officer and finishing my law degree. I passed the written test or assessment and I was invited for the oral assessment process. My oral assessment took place in San Juan, Puerto Rico.

I perceived the oral assessment at that time as being very culturally oriented in the sense that unless you had a particular social and ethnic background you would have a very difficult time fathoming what it was all about. The one fact that blew my chances of being admitted to the Foreign Service was my stage fright: when I was asked to name three American artists that I would consider candidates for being designated as living monuments as in Japan, I, for some reason, could not come up with any names. I could only come up with the names of European artists. Why I floundered I cannot say, but I knew then as I know now dozens of American artists, ranging from actors to writers. At that time, they gave you a reason for the denial of your application. My reason was: "lack of creativity." Think about that; I who had worked the educational system to finish high school in three years and college in three years all by myself was classified as "lacking in creativity."

Well, that certainly doused my enthusiasm for the Foreign Service for a long time. I forgot about the idea of joining the Foreign Service for many years and I kept on living my life, finished my law degree and began working in my chosen profession as an attorney with the Department of Justice.

After the death of my grandfather, I was again ready to leave Puerto Rico. So, I made two separate applications. I made an application to be appointed an immigration judge and I again began the process to be appointed a Foreign Service Officer. Now, that might seem odd, but to me it made perfect sense since there were no sitting immigration judges in Puerto Rico, which meant leaving the island, and the Foreign Service meant, by definition, service abroad.

Life is never easy or unequivocal. I was appointed an immigration judge with a delayed start date and a postponed security clearance investigation for reasons having to do with the compensation package at the law firm I was working for. In the meanwhile, I got a phone call from a Foreign Service recruitment officer to start my oral assessment process. But sticking to commitments and principles has always been my hallmark. I was frank with the recruiter and I told him that I had made a commitment with the Department of Justice and I considered it improper and unethical to continue with the application process to join the Foreign Service, which would have meant an abbreviated tenure as an immigration judge; and that was that. My second attempt to join the Foreign Service was trumped by the appointment as an immigration judge.

The third and final attempt to join the Foreign Service was a degree in life in itself. I was then an attorney in private practice in Miami, having resigned my employment as an immigration judge after four and a half years on the bench. I always considered my resignation from the bench to have been an existential decision that marked the rest of my life. The reasons for that decision were varied and not altogether consistent one with the other.

There is a procedure to engage in any new employment. The Foreign Service has always had its own multi-step recruitment process. I was familiar with the standard process of written examination, written essays and then the oral assessment. But I found out that there was at that time another process for persons with an established professional track record, the mid-level appointment process.

I figured I qualified to apply under that program since I had by then accumulated a total of 16 years of work as an attorney, seven of those years as a federal government employee in various legal capacities.

The mid-level appointment process was, in 1992, a mystery. Even finding out about its existence required a major research effort. But, I managed to get the details through serendipity.

I filed the paperwork to join the Foreign Service because a friend of mine, who had applied for employment in the Foreign Service under the Mid-level program and had succeeded in actually entering the service under that program, shared with me that the program existed and he informed me exactly which office to address the application to. Now, we are now talking about 1991 and I was not then familiar with the internet and I certainly had no personal knowledge of anyone in the State Department. Had he not given me the initial information, and be the good shepherd that he was in guiding me through the process and pointing outh the correct office at the

State Department to make the initial contact, I would have never joined the Foreign Service of the United States.

My first issue, even before I filed the initial application paperwork, was to solve family status issues. Entering the Foreign Service means being willing and able to relocate, and to relocate any place abroad, away from family and friends. If you are married, that means making sure your spouse is also willing and able to do so or, at the minimum, being willing to consider the possibility.

In my case, it was not that case when I began to consider joining the Foreign Service; my then wife resolutely rejected the possibility of life away from Miami. I asked in a roundabout way my then spouse on the issue of relocating. The answer was negative; she was not willing to relocate outside of the Miami area. The general tenor of the marital relationship was then very negative and one thing led to another. This conversation about relocation outside the Miami area precipitated the dormant issues arising from an initial mismatch that was not corrected previously on account of deep religious considerations.

It would be inaccurate to say that the Foreign Service caused my divorce since when I divorced I had not even yet filed the initial application paperwork. But not ending a failed marriage was a deterrent to considering any employment opportunity outside the Miami area. I submitted by initial paperwork for the Foreign Service about two weeks after the divorce was pronounced by the Circuit Court in Miami.

Life moved fairly fast for me at that time, as did my application to join the Foreign Service. My status as an eligible unmarried male was very brief. Before I had an appointment to present myself for the oral assessment, I had remarried. I married in February of 1992 and my oral assessment was in April, 1992. The issue of relocating abroad if the application succeeded was discussed prior to marriage and the response from my then fiancee was affirmative (she herself had lived in more than one country other than her own already).

This time, to my amazement, I breezed throught the oral assessment. I can only describe myself at the oral assessment as being on a roll. I just went from tranche to tranche of the oral assessment with a confidence in my abilities that even to this day surprises me. I chose the right subject for the written essay. I chose carefully the words in the group exercises. I showed the right amount of reticence in the one to one exercises. And, before that day was over, I was informed that I was hired, subject, of course, to necessary security and medical clearances.

The news to me, of course, was a joy. I had always dreamt of being a Foreign Service officer. On the other hand, the news to my new in-laws was a source of consternation. My in-laws thought that I had an end-job in Miami as a half-successful solo practitioner and that they, consequently, would have their daughter close by for the foreseeable future. I don't think they believed that my induction into the Foreign Service would come through when I mentioned the subject prior to my marriage to their daughter, but it did.

My medical examinations and assessments went without a hitch. My security clearance also came through without a hitch; I think it came through quickly partly because it was more of an update, given my recent service as an immigration judge in Miami. And, in October 1992, I was asked to choose a date to begin my training at the Foreign Service Institute. I was given two options. I chose the option that had me in the service at the earliest possible opportunity: January 2, 1993.

Since at the time we had to give to the Foreign Service our household effects and we had been married less than a year, we still had two separate homes. Since my separate home was a beach condominium, we spent the week at her home and the weekend in my home. Giving our household goods to the Foreign Service for indefinite storage was the first time my wife and I had our separate household goods commingled.

The process did not go smoothly. The movers the State Department had hired to pack and move our household goods were sloppy, untimely and rude. I had them cease the packing and I called the contact person at the Foreign Service and they actually listened and sent a totally different crew to finish the packing and carting away of our household goods. Thus ended our life in Miami in preparation to join the Foreign Service.

The process was not without a heavy emotional overlay. On the one hand, it was a dream come true to me and a reprieve from a faltering law practice. On the other hand, eight years of living and working in Miami had given me a very supportive network. Although my wife was accustomed to moving and a starting all over again, this time around she was going to a city where she would not have relatives close by. On that less than wholeheartedly cheerful note we trekked to Washington, D.C. on January 1, 1993.

The Foreign Service Institute

With nothing but your suitcase, you feel really up in the air. Both of our homes were totally empty and up for rent. We moved for a couple of days with my in-laws while the day to departure for Washington, DC came. Our departure from Miami was on January 1, 1993.

I must admit that everything went fairly smoothly about finding a furnished apartment in the Washington area within the per diem allowance of the Foreign Service. We managed to contract for the apartment by telephone and fax and we moved straight into the rented apartment from the airport. Even though it was not our furniture, we were glad we were again in a place we could call home, even if temporarily.

I entered the Foreign Service Insitute on January 2, 1993. It was a cold and snowy winter morning. I took the metro from the apartment to the Foreign Service Institute. My prior stays in the DC area served me well since I could navigate the city like a native, which in a sense I was after two separate stints living in the city.

I joined in the 66th entering class of the Foregin Service Institute since its reorganization. I was not the oldest entering officer candidate, that distinction belonged to a female officer, but I think I was the one with the most varied pre-Foreign Service experience. The next five months proved to be one of the most intensive learing periods in my life, and I loved it.

We had classroom work, we had homework, we had field trips and we had bonding exercises. It was fun being with a group of intellingent and very motivated people trying to do the best in order to get a good first assignment abroad. I, of course, was very much into the exercise of restrained competition. But little did I know that the powers that be had chosen already my first assignment abroad even before I had finished the second month of training at the Foreign Service Institute. But more about that later.

The classroom work at the Institute was the typical exercise you would expect at any college level learning institution in the United States. Although the dress code was relaxed, the discipline was not. We were expected to, and we all in fact did, arrive on time for classes. The homework was not exhausting, but it certainly was not a piece of cake and woe to him who did not produce it when requested. But we had good research facilities at our disposal to do it and it was fun to use those state of the art facilities.

The field trips were preparatory for our later work. One of the field trips that I most remember was the one to the District of Columbia morgue to familiarize us with that type of facility. One of the more trying chores of American Foreign Service Officers abroad is to assist with the identification of bodies of deceased American citizens and make the necessary arrangements for final disposition of the remains, be it in the United States or abroad when relatives are not on site to do so. Obviously, the powers that be thought best to desentize us to dead bodies in a controlled setting. But I soon found out that morgues in less developed countries are not the D.C. morgue.

Since I did not need language training for my first assignment (to Venezuela), I was ready to ship out to post in April 1993. However, that did not pan out with the assignment to post process and I had, basically, two months with little to do at the Institute. So, it was not hard for me to convince the training coordinator assigned to me to enroll me in language training—French. I had scored just below the professional proficiency level in French when I was examined upon entering the Foreign Service. I just needed some training in pronunciation and cultural references to reach the required professional level proficiency. After six weeks of French language training, I was certified qualified in French at the professional level.

I did not know then that the whole assignment process was, as far as my particular case was concerned, a charade, until I was at post. I eagerly submitted my list of posts and had long conversations with my wife concerning the ones she liked more and long conversations with my career counsellor about which one would be best for my career path. We wound up deciding Caracas would be best. I was not told I was going to Caracas until April, 1993. After arrival at post, I found an internal document in the files of the Consular Section of the American Embassy in Caracas in which, some time in February 1993, they were discussing the fact that they had found the replacement for the American Citizen Services officer who had unexpectedly departed Caracas, and retired, after his first morgue visit.

That memo should not have upset me. Anyway, Caracas was my first choice. However, after finding that memo I wondered whether the list that was given to me (and it was not a regular list since I was the only mid-level officer in that entering class) was simply concocted, not truly representative of available posts abroad and skewed to make me make the selection they wanted as the outcome. I will never know but the suspicion that it was is supported by all the circumstancial evidence.

Life in the Foreign Service

Foreign Service life is akin to life as an officer in the armed forces. One has a presidential commission like an armed forces officer. One has the aura that surrounds being an Officer of the United States. That is an ego booster in any league.

Furthermore, one is really an officer. The work one is called to involves the execution of policy in a very real and immediate manner and it involves right from the beginning the supervision of others; initially one supervises foreign national employees at the posts and soon thereafter, probably as early as the second tour of duty if one has the innate aptitude for the task, other foreign service officers. But, on the other hand, there is also the discipne of being an officer.

The best part of life in the Foreign Service is when one is posted abroad. First, economically it is quite a deal. The government pays for your housing and your utility bills (except telephone). Your salary is only for your food, clothing and incidentals and transportation. Furthermore, if anything goes bad in your housing, you simply call the administrative offices of the post and they will take care of it, at no cost to you (except in the rare instance when they determine you were at fault for the mishap). Many take the opportunity to save for the time when they return on assignment to the United States.

When you are back in the United States, you simply become another civil service employee. You retain the title of Foreign Service officer, but you have to manage your life like any other employee for any employer. And, when you return one of your immediate tasks, on your own, is to find and contract for housing. After being taken care of so well, it is quite a shocker for many.

Abroad, you have a very active social life. Everyone abroad wants to say they have a friend at the American Embassy. So, you will receive a constant stream of invitations for every conceivable event. Some of them are obligatory (those involving official functions involving your contacts in the host government), others are optional (most of the invitations received from other missions accredited to the country) and others are no-nos (those are becoming rarer every day; usually you are allowed to go with the proviso that you will file a detailed report of what went on and what were you asked). But you will receive guidance from your supervisor as to the categories; the real issue for one is how much time does one wants for oneself.

Back in Washington, again you are simply another civil servant. Unless you have a high visibility job, you will be ignored socially by everyone. You will have to rely for socialization on your family, your before-Foreign Service friends, the fellow Foreign Service friends you made abroad if you are lucky enough to be assigned concurrently to Washington and your fellow coworkers, if you happen to like one another. However, one thing you do learn in the Foreign Service is how to break the ice and start a conversation.

Another issue that is irksome to some is the intrusiveness of the service into your health. Before you are assigned to any post abroad, you must be medically cleared for that post. The general state of your your health will play a big role in which assignments you can request for yourself. The medical facilities in the country that you will be assigned must be sophisticated enough to cover your health needs. If you have a chronic condition that is deemed not treatable in a particular country, you will not be assigned to that country. This means that before you are cleared to go to a particular country you will be examined exhaustively by a Foreign Service physician that will go through your medical history in detail. And it is really in detail, going into your drinking, smoking, eating and other habits. It is part of the package.

After I joined the Foreign Service, I developed a chronic condition. The condition, with proper follow up, is not disabling and the required treatment is considered rather routine. However, periodic testing and treatment is required to avoid complications. Every time I was about to change posts, regardless of how recently I had gone through the rather intrusive testing, I had to go through it again to ascertain the status of the condition. The condition never prevented me from being assigned to any post I wanted, but the testing was no fun.

Another plus of being abroad is that if you have to be hospitalized, the tab is entirely covered by the Foreign Service, with or without insurance. If you have insurance, you will be asked to file a claim and assign the benefits to the government; the balance is not your responsibility. Now, that is not an excuse not to have medical insurance. As soon as you are out of the country of assignment, any medical bill, including hospitalization, is your responsibility. So, unless you intend not to depart the country of assignment for any reason during your tour of duty (a very unlikely scenario) and you have excellent health, you are well advised to have medical insurance.

Once you back in the United States, again you are simply another civil service employee. Your health is your responsibility, as it should be. You have access, like any other federal employee, to the group health plans available to all federal employees.

For those with school age children, the deal is even more all-inclusive. The government will pay for private school in English through high school in the country of assignment. If the country of assignment does not have appropriate facilities for this, you will have the option of sending your children to boarding school in the United States or another convenient foreign country.

Again, when you are back in the United States, your children's education is your responsibility.

A little known benefit for people in the Foreign Service is the ability to keep their domestic servants engaged abroad when they return to the United States. You have to pay them American wages when they work for you in the United States, but they get a special visa that allows them to work for you because you are deemed to have your principal place of employment abroad and to be only temporarily in the United States when you are assigned to the Department of State.

Arrival at post of first assignment

Nothing happens the way it is planned. Arrival at my first post of assignment was no exception. Although my arrival schedule was meticulously documented by standard State Department telecommunications, the person that was supposed to greet me at the airport upon my arrival was . . . not there. Since he was not there, I had no local currency and no Venezuelan cell phone, I had to beg a stranger the use of a telephone to call the American Embassy and get in touch with my designated greeter. Upon contact, he was very apologetic. The end result was a couple of hours at the Maiquetìa airport with my wife and baggage in tow until such time as he arrived. We looked and felt more like displaced refugees than persons arriving on an official mission.

My greeter, a very nice and congenial mid-level officer with whom later I developed a good friendship, took us directly to the furnished apartment that had been rented by the embassy for my wife and myself. Although the apartment was huge (I was hired as a mid-level officer with the expectation that I would do official entertainment), it certainly was not overflowing with amenities. We soon discovered that one of the necessities of modern urban life, running water, was in short supply at the building and that we had to more or less schedule our lives around water flow hours. Welcome to Caracas.

We settled in the apartment, got to know the building superintendent (a very kind and helpful man from a third country) and the immediate neighbors and I began my work as an American Foreign Service Officer accredited to a foreign country. Little did I know at that point in time that I was in for an exciting, albeit exhausting, two years abroad. I began my life in Caracas with a sense of having arrived. In a very practical and immediate way, I had.

I soon learned that your success as a Consular Officer in the Foreign Service is dependent on the so-called foreign service national employees. These are the local support employees, from very menial laborers to very astute and capable professionals, that are hired by American embassies abroad to give continuity to the work at hand and preserve a certain institutional local memory. We must remember that the normal tour of duty of a Foreign Service officer in the American Foreign Service is on average less than three years. Although everything that transpires is documented in exhausting detail by regular and punctilious communications with the Department of State, it is simply impossible for new arrivals to learn all there is to learn about the local realities and pitfalls before making the first serious blunder in the country.

My first test of character in Venezuela was the visit to the local morgue to identify the remains of a deceased American citizen. Morgues in most Latin American countries do not have refrigeration facilities. Consequently, the stench of decomposing bodies is overwhelming. Furthermore, the lack of such facilities makes it imperative that formalities, and arranging for corpse pick-up, be a time sensitive task. Since my only previous morgue experience was the visit to the District of Columbia morgue during my Foreign Service training, I was really not ready for this experience.

But I survived. I identified the body from the photograph in the passport which the police had at hand and I returned to the embassy to make the necessary contacts to inform relatives of the death of their relative and to ascertain their wishes concerning the disposition of the remains. Everything went smoothly and the body was repatriated for burial in the United States through the services of a local funeral home known to the embassy.

As I mentioned earlier, my immediate predecessor in the position of American Citizen Services officer had departed post immediately after his first morgue visit. He had the years of service and decided to retire instead of going through morgue visits for two years. Upon my arrival in Caracas, since I was a mid-level officer and it was not generally known to local employees that I had just been hired into the Foreign Service, one of the first questions that the chief Venezuelan support employee at the section asked me was if I was eligible to retire!

The chief Venezuelan support employee at the Consular Section was an impressive person. She had made the American Embassy her life. Since she was so knowledgeable about her work and the environment, it was natural to defer to her whenever different courses of action were presented. I soon learned that it was temerary not to follow her recommendations and I, like all my predecessors and successors, found it useful to go with her flow.

But that deference to a subordinate has its pitfalls, as I soon found out. The issue that brought it home was the necessity to fire an underperforming support employee. She recommended the firing, gave me a detailed report of the failings of the employee and advised me of the costs involved in firing the person. It all sounded very reasonable and I called in the employee for the exit interview.

Well, the employee did not take it lying down. She refuted the allegations of subpar performance and flatly stated that she saw no reason to speak with me since the real decision maker was the chief support employee. Luckily, she was not the first employee I had to fire in my life; I had had my own law practice and had fired more than one support employee.

I stood my grown and said that the decision had been made, that I was the person with final authority over her continuation or not in her employment and that she was fired. She was escorted to the Embassy's personnel office and—I never heard anything more from her.

But the entire episode reminded me that one has to take a personal and immediate interest right from the beginning as to the performance of all employees under one's supervision and that face to face discussions of periodic assessments are a must. Furthermore, firing an employee on subpar performance grounds too soon after one's arrival is not good policy since one is making a decision based solely on somebody else's appraisal and Foreign Service Officers should never be seen as being mere rubber stamps.

Prison Visits

One of the items of constant work at the Consular Section of the American Embassy in Caracas was the required periodic visits to American citizens incarcerated in Venezuelan jails. When I arrived at post, almost the entirety of that prison population was incarcerated on account of drug trafficking charges. Invariably, they had been provided a free junket to Venezuela and the border area with Colombia by a real full time trafficker in exchange for the transportation of a couple of kilos of cocaine to the United States. Of course, Venezuelan authorities were very much aware of this trafficking and they had a very good handle on the profiles. And, when these accidental trafffickers were caught, they all pleaded complete innocence and blustered that they could not fathom how the cocaine got into their luggage or other possessions. Not one of them ever acknowledged to me guilt, even after conviction by Venezuelan courts.

Venezuelan prison sentences for possession with intent to distribute drugs at that time were stiff and even handedly applied. Almost always the judge imposed on the poor soul a fifteen-year prison sentence. However, most convicts only served approximately half of the sentence given the then generous provisions of the Venezuelan penal code for credits for good behavior. Good behavior was not hard to perform since bad behavior was severely punished by strict prison authorities who gleefully meted out physical pain at the slightest provocation.

The one item that caused a lot of official grief and concern at the American Embassy and at the State Department was the lack of food for inmates in Venezuelan prisons. Although the Venezuelan state ostensibly fed its prison inmate population, in practice the funds at that time were habitually stolen by prison officials (except at model prisons where high profile convicts were housed) and the inmates were required, by hook or crook, to find food to eat.

Since this was common knowledge, there was then a very liberal visitation program for inmates. Family members of local inmates would come twice a week to bring food to their relatives. American citizens, however, being away from their home country and thus their relatives, had it really hard. The United States Government finally made the decision, long before my arrival in Venezuela, to provide incarcerated American citizens in Venezuela with periodic funds to assist them in purchasing food. This was done through a loan program that was to be repaid at some point in time after the citizen's return to the United States.

The logistics of disbursement were very time consuming. Every quarter a request for funds had to be made to the Department of State for each and every inmate individually. Once approved, the funds had to be converted into the local currency and personally delivered to the inmate by consular officials. At the time of disbursement, the inmate would sign a promissory note in favor of the United States Government to be repaid upon return to the United States.

American citizens were not housed in a central penitenciary. They were generally imprisoned in a prison close to the place where they were apprehended. Venezuela is dotted with jails east and west, north and south. American consular officers in Venezuela, especially the American Citizens Services officers, had a really trying permanent travel schedule. Since I was the American Citizens Services officer in Venezuela, I spend two years traveling on average twice a week throughout Venezuela. It was fun at the beginning but the novelty soon wore off. Since I speak impeccable Spanish, I was usually sent alone by the Consul General to make the prison visits.

The logistics of travel were demanding. Since the Venezuelan road system outside of Caracas and the nearby towns was rudimentary, the only way to visit outlying jails without making it a three or four day outing was to fly to the nearest city with an airport and then . . . hail a cab. I was lucky in that I could, and did, pass as a Venezuelan visiting a friend, relative or client in jail. So, generally speaking, I was not taken too much advantage of by taxi drivers and others who had to provide the necessary transportation services to the jails. Now I say others because in some places the transport was not exactly a taxi, as would be recognized in the United States. I marvel at the fact that I was never kidnapped or held up during those two years of constant solo travel in the hinterland of Venezuela.

My two years in Venezuela had a very salutary effect in the American inmate population in that country. Not a single American citizen died a violent death in Venezuelan jails during my two years in that country. Prior to my arrival and after my departure violent deaths of incarcerated American citizens was a constant headache to the Department of State. I am proud of my accomplishment, an accomplishment that was recognized by the Department of State by a Superior Honor Award for my work on behalf of incarcerated American citizens in Venezuelan jails.

Some Warden

Some Venezuelan prison wardens were very conscientious persons who tried to do their job to the best of their abilities. Some even had some empathy for the inmates in their care. Some others, however, could only be described as demented psychopaths who took every opportunity to show who the boss was and inflict all sorts of demeaning actions on the inmates and impose severe physical punishment on the least provocation.

Although one hates to badmouth anyone, one particular warden has remained in my mind after so many years after my departure from Venezuela. He was the warden of a jail far away from Caracas and far away from anyone that could exercise minimal supervision over his comings and goings. Fortunately for my fellow citizens incarcerated in his facility, I manage to strike a cordial relationship with him which resulted in no American citizen being murdered there (prior to my arrival, a number of incarcerated American citizens had been murdered and it was rumored that he may have had a hand in the matter and he certainly made no effort to prevent murders in the jail).

The shocking conversation with him that I will never forget was concerning prison breakouts. One day I arrived at the prison and he was very agitated and readying his weapons. He told me that he had confidential information that a breakout was about to occur and that he was . . . ready for them. It was obvious from the glint in his eyes that he was looking forward to the thrill of the chase. Luckily for the escapees, they did not try to escape that day (had they found out he was ready for them?).

Later I learned from him that sometimes he would relax perimeter surveillance to allow prisoners to attempt escaping. Then, he would go after them and round them up to show the inmates that escape was impossible. And, if some died while he tried to capture them and bring them back . . . well, too bad for them, they asked for it.

This same warden did something one day that really showed me how callous he was. One day when I was leaving the prison there was a sale of artifacts manufactured by inmates going on. The artifacts were really of mediocre quality, but they brought the inmates enough cash to pay for their food. When we were going by one stand, he simply plucked one of the artifacts and handed it over to me as a memento of my visit. I protested that I wanted to pay, but he told the inmate in a very inequivocal tone "You wanted to give it to the consul, didn't you." I just felt as dehumanized as the inmate.

Socializing with him was tough on my conscience. But I knew that if I did not do it, innocent persons could die for no reason at all. So, whenever I went to this prison I would make it a point to pay a personal call on him at his office after visiting detained citizens. Furthermore, I would go to lunch with him; sometimes I paid for lunch some others he did so as to avoid in his mind any suspicion that I was trying to bribe him.

A plane causes grief to its pilot

This is one of the most incredible experiences I had ever encountered and the persons involved, although very likely no angels, could not be rightly convicted by the Venezuelan authorities under any reasonable standard of proof. They were finally convicted of a made up crime so as not to have to return the money found in the plane piloted by the American defendant that was stolen by someone in the police headquarters during the pendency of the criminal proceedings.

This American citizen arrived in Venezuela in a private twin engine plane. He and everyone else agreed that he landed at Maiquetìa airport (the airport serving Caracas) on account of mechanical difficulties. Upon inspection of the plane, the authorities found . . . half a million dollars in cash. The plot immediately began to thicken.

The officers who inspected the plane and found the cash called their headquarters in Caracas. Upon contact with headquarters, the officer in charge of that police contingent at the airport was instructed to take no further action that the chief of the service would personally go down to the airport to deal with the matter. Which he did to the chagrin of the American citizen.

The chief of that police division was very blund and straightforward. He told the American citizen either you leave the half million dollars and you can walk away or you will still leave the half million dollars and you will stay in jail for a long time while we find a suitable crime to allow us to confiscate the money. Choice one was the correct choice. But, people being so used to Hollywood endings where justice prevails and the good live happily ever after, my future ward decided to chose option number two.

Of course, the innocent private pilot had a plausible explanation for the half million dollars in his plane. And yes, nobody believed him. He stated that the money was to buy jewelry in Curacao and that he would get a better price if he paid cash (had he ever heard of wire transfers?). Granted, this was before September 11, 2001. The Venezuelans suspected otherwise, specifically that the money was to buy drugs to transport back to the United States.

Of course, the Venezuelan police officer was true to his promise. He was duly booked for drug trafficking with no evidence of drugs and, later, money laundering added as an afterthought. The money was taken into police custody and the custodian, voila, was the chief of the contigent who put the money in the safe in his office, ostensibly as evidence of the crime.

Does it surprise you that the money was stolen from the police chief's office safe? If it does, you believe in Hollywood endings and that law enforcement officers do their duty all the time and that they are there everywhere to serve and protect. Now, I don't say that doesn't ever happen in Venezuela. However, in Venezuela in the 1980's and 1990's to believe that was the norm was to have a lot of faith in fairy tales.

Well, another problem with the Venezuelan justice system at the time was that it took forever to any case to be brought to conclusion. Over one half of detained persons in Venezuelan prisons at that time were awaiting conviction and sentencing. My twin engine pilot spent ten years waiting for a final judicial determination on his case. He finally got his sentence for . . . five years. The crime he was convicted of was failure to declare funds upon arrival in the country. He served twice the sentence and there was a legal basis to forfeit the funds. The chief of police was true to his word—you will never see that money again.

Boats can be arrested

This would be a charming story if it were not for the fact that what gave rise to the action was the tragic death by suicide of a youth. The death occurred when the student in a school ship that docked at La Guaira, under the influence of drugs, decided to jump to his death from the ship to the dock. He landed head first in the quay where the ship was docked.

Normally, this would lead to the usual notice to the next of kin and the necessary arrangement to ship the body for burial in the United States. However, life is certainly stranger than fiction. Nothing went by the book right from the beginning and the plot thickened considerably before the right actions were taken.

Almost immediately after the death the embassy received confidential information to the effect that drugs were being abused by the students in the ship with the knowledge and possibly participation of the persons who were *in loco parentis*. We were also told that the deceased student kept a diary and that in this diary he had recorded his experiences of drug use, and with a certain detail as to places, times, companions, etc. This diary became a very powerful motivator to obstruct the normal procedures.

Now, the 1963 Vienna Convention on Consular Relations stipulates that when a foreign citizen dies without relatives in a foreign country the consul of his nationality has the right and duty to take possession of the personal belongings of the deceased for safekeeping until such time as arrangements are made with the next of kin for their disposal.[2] The death having occurred in Venezuela, the ship being docked in a Venezuelan port and there being

---

[2]   Article 5 (g) of the Convention provides that among the consular functions are: safeguarding the interests of nationals, both individuals and bodies corporate, of the sending States in cases of succession *mortis causa* in the territory of the receiving State, in accordance with the laws and regulations of the receiving State.

no next of kin of the deceased present, yours truly was duty bound to take possession of the personal belongings of the deceased, including the diary.

So, up I went into the ship and spoke with the captain of the ship and he refused to hand over the personal belongings of the deceased student to me. At first he was very polite, but as I continued to be insistent on the issue he became less and less polite. It is never a good idea not to be polite to a diplomatic agent. Frustrated, I decided to abandon the ship and head straight to the captain of the port to seek the assistance of the Venezuelan authorities to exercise my right to take possession of the deceased's personal belongings in accordance with international law, which binded not only the United States and Venezuela, but also the country of the ship's flag.

Well, it so happened that the captain of the port was not an unknown person to me. Now, I did not realize this until after I had walked into his office since my prior dealings with him had nothing to do with ports and boats, but with visas and vacation travel to the United States by him and his family members. That made for a very receptive captain of the port, who wanted to reciprocate the goodwill of the consular officer who had given him no trouble in getting visas for an unexpected family trip to the United States.

I gave the captain of the port all the details and I stressed to him that the applicable international convention was binding on all the countries involved and that I was simply asking for something that there was absolutely no question I was entitled to. Convinced of my arguments, he immediately ordered two port policemen to go with me to the boat and inform the captain of the ship that "the boat is arrested until such time as it is released by Consul Bracete." That may have been one of the most powerful moments in my life.

Well, the captain of the ship was not going to take it without a fight. He called his company's attorneys, who contacted legal counsel in Washington, DC, who then contacted the Department of State. The Department of State in turn called the embassy in Caracas and a frantic Consul General got me on a cell phone and asked me what I was doing. My gut reaction was to tell him that I had decided to start a full fledged diplomatic incident, but having then still a wish to remain in the Foreign Service until retirement, I chose instead to give him a detailed chronology of events, emphasizing that the decision to arrest the boat was made by the captain of the port and not by me. Well, his reaction, and excuse the vernacular, was: "you really have balls." I had never doubted I had them.

About five minutes before the scheduled departure time of the ship, and realizing that he would have to pay additional wharfage fees if he did not give up the personal belongings of the deceased student, the captain of the ship relented (caved-in?) and sent a message to the captaincy of the port to have me go up, that they were doing the inventory to hand over to me the personal belongings of the deceased student. This must certainly have been the swifted release of an arrested ship in history. I executed a handwritten document authorizing the ship's sailing and it sailed to its next port of call to be some other U.S. Consul's problem (most of the students on board were American and, if the confidential information we had was true, more problems were bound to arise before that sailing was over).

This proved a memorable event in the annals of the port, as it soon became apparent when other deaths of passengers on ships calling at port occurred subsequently. Cruise ships regularly called at La Guaira (the port servicing Caracas) with plenty of American tourists on board. A considerable portion of that tourist population is elderly, not used to strenuous exercise or tropical weather and cuisine. Inevitably, deaths by preventable causes do occur.

The next death of a cruise passenger that came to my attention proved the point. Upon learning of the death of the passenger, I called the ship' chief purser and I followed the standard routine of informing him who I was, what the law was and that I was required to take possession of the personal belongings of the deceased and they had the obligation of handing them over to me. Well, upon initial contact, that chief purser almost laughed me off the phone.

While pondering how to proceed, I received an unexpected return phone call from the chief purser asking me to please come down to the ship and pick up the personal effects of the deceased passenger. Obviously the ship's chandler brought the chief purser up to date that there was a consular officer that could, and would, arrest any ship to get the personal belongings of deceased American citizens if they were not traveling with a relative. There was never any further question of procedure in these eventualities after that.

An unsual notarial

American consular officers exercise notarial functions abroad for documents to be used in the United States. This has been a part of Foreign Service practice right from the beginning of the Republic and it comes from a history of long practice in international law. The power of American consular officers to perform notarial acts for documents to be used in the United States is codified in the law and it is one of the attributes of consular officers specifically recognized in the 1963 Vienna Convention on Consular Relations.[3] As the Chief of American Citizen Services, I had primary responsibility for notarial activity in Venezuela, after the Consul General, of course.

Once upon a time there were two presidents of Venezuela at the same time. One of them was in the Miraflores Presidential Palace as Acting President and the other one was in his private home under house arrest. One day, a request came from the president under house arrest, Carlos Andrés Pérez, requesting a consular officer to perform a notarial act for a document to be used in the United States. The issue for the American Embassy became one of protocol. The country team (all senior officers in the American Embassy in the country) had to decide whom to send.

This was an exercise in fine tuning relations with the host government. The Embassy could not send just a junior consular officer to do the notarial since it could be considered a slight, given that the president in house arrest was still technically the president of the country, even though he was prevented from exercising his functions. Sending the Consul General to do the notarial could be construed as a political statement as to the removal from effective office of the elected president. So, yours truly, a mid-level officer,

---

[3]   Article 5 (g) of the Convention provides that among the consular functions are: acting as notary and civil registrar and in capacities of a similar kind, and performing certain functions of an administrative nature, provided that there is nothing contrary thereto in the laws and regulations of the receiving State.

was sent to take the oath of Carlos Andrés Pérez, Constitutional President of Venezuela under house arrest.

Carlos Andrés Pérez was truly gracious. I was ushered into his presence by the army of bodyguards surrounding him. Since I had already received a copy of the document to be notarized, the actual episode was brief and uneventful. That was the only time I saw Carlos Andrés Pérez.

Crime in the city

Venezuela at that time had a serious crime situation. We were constantly reminded of that fact by the security personnel at the embassy. We were encouraged to avoid travel at night, even within the city of Caracas.

It so happened that one night I just could not abide by the recommendation because my wife was returning from the United States and I had to go and pick her up at the airport. It was twilight. I got out of the residential building's parking lot and about a few blocks from my apartment I noticed I was being followed. Following procedures taught to us as part of the security training prior to being posted abroad, I managed to lose my follower and I headed home by a different route. Upon arrival at the apartment, I notified the embassy security officer of the incident and an official vehicle was provided to pick up my wife at the airport.

Another time, coming come from the embassy after a long day, I was, like all denizens of Caracas at rush hour, immersed in bumper to bumper traffic that moved with the speed of sleepy camels at twilight. Right in front of me, a group of armed hoodlums approached the driver of the car in front of me and robbed him at gunpoint. Being unarmed, there was nothing I could do. After they left, my reaction was, but for the grace of God, that victim could have been me.

Another sorry incident was the carjacking of my neighbor's car. Returning from work, husband, wife and kids stopped at a nearby bakery to buy bread. The husband left the car running for the air conditioning since his wife and two daughters were in the car. An armed person entered and was about to take off with all of them in the car.

Well, my neighbor had a lot of self control. She told the robber that it was fine for him to take the car (who can argue with an armed person), but he could not take the two girls with him. It worked. He allowed the three women to get off the car. The car, with diplomatic plates, was never seen again.

Another incredible event of bold petty theft must be mentioned. My wife was joining me to a trip to Cartagena, Colombia. This trip had been arranged by the association of consular officers in Venezuela. At the airline counter, she handed handed over her passport and the plane ticket. She lost eye contact momentarily with the counter agent and when she regained eye contact with him he again asked her for the plane ticket.

Taken aback, she told him that she had just handed him over the ticket with her passport, which was in plain view. Well, he was adamant about the fact that she had not delivered the plane ticket and insisted that she must buy a new plane ticket if she wanted to proceed to the boarding gate. Faced with the possibility of missing the flight, she purchased a new ticket. Efforts later through the American Embassy to get a refund for the stolen airplane ticket proved fruitless. Welcome to Venezuela.

Persona non grata

One of the possibilities of a Foreign Service officer doing his work diligently is being declared by the host government persona non grata. I never thought that would be an issue since the work I did abroad as a Foreign Service officer was totally unrelated to politics or covert opetrations. But even the most innocuous things have a way of evolving into controversial issues at any time.

One of the duties of consular officers abroad is to look after the welfare of American citizens, especially those that are incarcerated, hospitalized, under a disability or who are minors. If they are incarcerated, hospitalized or under a disability, the host government usually is relieved that someone else is taking care of the problem.

When it comes to minors, especially minors with dual nationality or whose parents are dual nationals or one is a local and the other an American, they would rather you not show up at all. I got caught up in one of these.

As routinely happens, the Department of State received a request from the American parent residing in the United States asking for a welfare and whereabouts as to his child in Venezuela in the custody of the Venezuelan parent. As Chief of the American Citizen Services Unit in Venezuela, I was the officer with primary responsibility to take action on the request from the Department of State as to welfare and whereabouts of citizens.

Following standard practice, I ascertained the whereabouts of the child and proceeded to go to his home to ascertain the state of his welfare. Again, following standard practice, I made my presence known to the local police chief and requested that one of his officers accompany me to visit the child's home. They agreed to come with me and I interviewed the child who appeared to be in good health and well taken care of. I left the home of the child, returned to the embassy and filed my report with the Department of State. As far as I was concerned at that moment, that was the end of it.

Well, nothing is simple when children are involved. Two days later a full page article appeared in one of the major local newspapers accusing me of plotting to kidnap the child back to the United States and demanding that the Venezuelan government immediately declared me persona non grata and expelled me from the country. I was totally surprised by this and thought to myself what a way to begin one's Foreign Service career.

The reaction of my superiors was totally unexpected to me. They laughed their heads off. First, they indicated to me that I would not be the first Foreign Service officer to be declared *persona non grata* over a minor issue and that it actually was a reputation enhancer to be declared *persona non grata* at least once in one's career. Lastly, they predicted that the Venezuelan government, given my careful planning in performing the welfare and whereabouts check, would not ask for my removal from the country. They were right; I finished my tour of duty as scheduled.

How I got
my second assignment

Chance, or the luck of the draw, is an integral part of life, as Nassim Taleb would say. We can certainly help our chances of getting something by assiduously working every angle that leads to the goal, but, ultimately, chance has a lot to do with what one gets out of life. How I got my second assignment to be a consular officer in the country of my wife's birth and nationality was chance, pure and simple.

It was then part of the Foreign Service routine to schedule regional seminars for consular officers posted in the region. Every post in the region would choose an officer to represent the post at the regional meeting. By the time the regional meeting of 1994 was convened, I was already about halfway into my tour of duty in Venezuela, had a good relationship with my supervisor, the consul general, and it was thus natural for me to be selected to represent the post at the regional seminar. Since my wife wanted to go along, I took her at my own cost and expense since dependents were never included in travel orders for this type of event.

Besides being an opportunity to compare notes on regional issues, the seminars promoted the desired esprit de corps among the officers in the field, that is a necessary ingredient to make an ultimately interpersonal relations job be fruitful. Additionally, it allows the powers that be in Washington to mingle with the rank and file in a fairly open and level environment. I suspect this mingling by high ranking officials from Washington had a lot to do with identifying candidates to serve in the Department in sensitive administrative positions.

So, we mingled and nobody objected that my wife mingled at the social events that were scheduled. It turned out that the number two person in the Bureau of Consular Affairs, my control bureau, was the highest ranking official to come down from Washington for the Latin American Regional

Consular Seminar. She was a lovely lady, single, never married, whose only purpose in life was to be a Foreign Service Officer.

We hit it off pretty well. I was not eligible for a Washington assignment since new officers are expected to do two tours abroad and then be considered for a Washington assignment. I was not looking for a Washington assignment anyway (the way the Foreign Service is set up, you actually get a pay cut when assigned to Washington). So the fact that I invited her for dinner with my wife was seen as a purely friendly gesture on my part and she accepted the invitation in the same vein.

After getting better acquainted with each other, my wife and I dutifully asked her about her experiences in the Foreign Service. She had a lot of truly great stories. Unfortunately for me, the only interesting bit of information I retained from her that evening was the etimoloy of Istambul, the Turkish name of the Byzantine capital. She had been assigned to Turkey at some point in her Foreign Service career. The name Istambul in the original language of the times means basically the place there; although the way she explained it, which unfortunately I cannot recall, was marvelous.

Well, I guess out of civility she asked me where I wanted to go on my second assignment. I did not even have a chance to think before my wife chirped in: "my country, of course." Now, there is a certain disinclination on the part of all foreign services to send people on assignment to countries where they have emotional attachments, for obvious reasons. I was surprised by the response, a response that engraved in stone right then and there my next assignment: "that can be arranged." So, even thought it was far from bidding time for my next assignment, I knew then and there where I was going for my second assignment, El Salvador.

When the actual bidding process for my second assignment opened, El Salvador was right there on the list of available posts for onward assignment. I dutifully filled out the form, identifying the required number of choices and writing the narratives justifying why those choices were selected. Again, as for my first assignment, which was decided long before the bidding process was concluded, my second assignment was decided long before the bidding process was commenced.

Managing an encounter

The Foreign Service is like the military—you follow the orders of your superiors or face the consequences. Sometimes you can manage the consequences by proactive action. I was once faced with one of those situations where following the orders of your superior would have resulted in the commission of a serious fault and I had to do something not to face the equally disagreeable consequences of a charge of insubordination. But I managed.

Like everything in the Foreign Service, it happened on a Friday after clerical help had departed from the building and only eager beavers like myself were still at the job. A summer intern assigned to the ambassador came into my office, documents in hand, with the peremptory request that I notarize the documents signed by someone not in my presence. Well, law and regulations require that a consular officer must have the person whose signature he is notarizing appear before him and either sign the document in his presence or acknowledge having signed it previously. I looked up from what I was doing and flatly told him no.

He was taken aback by my response. He expected me to simply do as I was told since it was the ambassador who had given the order. He sprinted out of my office and I knew what the next move was going to be. To have the needed support to refuse this request and avoid consequences, I immediately rushed to my immediate supervisor's office and I explained to her all that had transpired.

Luckily, she was a stickler for rules and she fully backed my position. She was also certain that we had not heard the last on that issue. We patiently waited for the next emissary and he duly arrived in the person of the Deputy Chief of Mission.

Naturally, he took the offensive stating that I had refused a direct order from the ambassador to perform a ministerial act of importance to the mission. My supervisor stated that I had done the right thing since the law and regulations required the person whose signature is to be authenticated to be in the presence of the consular officer to acknowledge his signature and this person whose signature was to be notarized was not at the embassy.

Given the solidarity shown by my supervisor, which meant that there was no way that authentication would be done in contravention of the regulations, he then asked what could be done to have the document authenticated immediately since it was in the government's interest that that document, duly authenticated, leave the country by diplomatic pouch. Well, we offered that I could go to the office of the person who signed the documents and take his acknowledgement face to face, which I actually did.

That intern never came back by my office during his remaining summer tour of duty at the embassy and the ambassador involved always made a point of greeting me whenever we happened to be in the same room. Having a backbone and good survival techniques certainly enhances your status in any organization.

Letter from Jumanji

When I was in the process of looking for my third assignment, I was looking for some excitement and also an opportunity to practice my French. Besides the obvious European posts (hard to get when you are a newly minted Foreign Service officer), there are posts in Africa and the Americas where you can use your French. Africa was out of the question, mostly on account of my wife's disinclination for too much excitement. So, the options were fairly narrow. One of the options available was Port au Prince in Haiti, official language French.

When I mentioned that I was interested in Haiti, my midlevel consular colleague at the Embassy in San Salvador asked me if I knew if the current incumbent of the position was not extending and if not why not. I think she was gently telling me that Haiti maybe was not the best option for my next assignment. I think she knew more than what she was letting me on.

So I did contact the incumbent. And I got an earful. Her e-mail in response to my friendly inquiry was about three pages long (the incumbent had been a journalist prior to joining the Foreign Service). Her three pages, which I printed and still retain, are a literary gem. In these three pages she described life for her in Port au Prince outside the office environment. The description was extraordinarily detailed and her cat was one of her heroes for taking on a number of vermin in her home, on a regular basis. Her last sentence in the e-mail was: "Extend my assignment? No, life is too short."

After reading the document, I certainly discarded the idea of going to Haiti on my third assignment, or any other assignment. But making the inquiry resulted in my acquiring a veritable literary gem that forever will be knows as the *Letter from Jumanji*.

My equivocations that led to my third assignment

I have to admit that towards the end of my second assignment I dithered as to whether or not to take an onward assignment. I toyed with the idea of leaving the Foreign Service, remain in El Salvador and build from scratch a finance company. Well, the whole episode was a fiasco for myself. I realized that I trusted people too much on very flimsy evidence.

Since my wife is Salvadoran, I had access to local businessmen in a way that was totally different from the access of other diplomats assigned to the country. Since I had been a bank officer prior to being an attorney, my profession immediately prior to my joining the Foreign Service, I had a fairly good idea of banking operations. El Salvador at that point in time had just come out of the civil war, and business opportunities were plentiful.

A fairly well to do expatriate Salvadoran wanted to invest in his home country. He was quite impressed with my credentials and my network in El Salvador and he proposed to put most of the capital for the new venture if I agreed to organize and lead it. It sounded a great idea at the time.

Contacts were made with other local potential investors and professionals to lead the enterprise. Since my assignment was coming to an end, there was a certain urgency to wrap up the loose ends, including work permits for me after departing the Foreign Service and actually giving notice to the Department of State that I was resigning. One thing that was left up in the air was the actual signing of the agreement to form the new venture.

Getting the work permit while still being a Foreign Service officer was tricky. But since the federal regulations allow an American citizen to keep his regular passport while in possession of a diplomatic passport issued upon entry into the Foreign Service, that allowed for the processing of the work permit through the Salvadoran system without need to bring up the issue of diplomatic status in the country.

Once the work permit was out of the way, but before any binding documents were signed by the provider of the capital, I presented my resignation from the Foreign Service with a delayed effective date, as is required by the guidelines and common sense since the Department of State has your personal belongings as hostages for compliance with the guidelines.

Less than a week after I presented my resignation from the Foreign Service, the expatriate Salvadoran investor renegued on his verbal commitment. His reasons were totally meritless, but let us not dwell on that. The issue was that I was up in the air: no future venture and no future employment.

I had to come back to the personnel officer at the Embassy and beg, hat in hand, that I be allowed to withdraw my letter of resignation. Surprisingly, the system did not make a fuss about allowing me to withdraw my letter of resignation. However, since I had presented the letter of resignation, my onward assignment had been cancelled and I was looking at a very uncomfortable period between the scheduled end of my tour and a new onward assignment.

God looks after children and dullards. Since I had economic expertise acquired from my undergraduate degree and my years in banking and a knack for writing, I was offered as my third assignment the position of Financial Economist in the Bureau of Economic Affairs. I departed El Salvador a chastened and wiser man to begin, what was to be, my last year of employment as a Foreign Service Officer.

My third assignment

During the last week of the home leave provided by regulations between assignments in the Foreign Service, I trekked to Washington, DC to look for housing. When in Washington, you are on your own as far as housing is concerned. Since we had to deal with the fact that one's furniture is delivered within 30 days of arrival at post in Washington, and we had the furniture of two houses to take delivery of, we needed a bit more of time than the allotted time to look for housing since we needed to rent a large house, not an apartment.

The process to look for housing was depressing. Good quality housing in or close to Washington itself is quite expensive. So, we had to look for a house outside the Beltway that we could afford and that would be big enough for our furniture to fit in. After more than three weeks looking, we found one. It was not the best location, but it would have to do.

My actual work environment at the Department of State was not bad. My office was in the Main State Building. I had a fairly sized office. Since I had to attend meetings on a regular basis at the Inter American Development Bank and the World Bank, it could not have been more convenient. I had the choice of walking to the meetings or taking a taxi, the choice depending usually on weather conditions.

Since my so called "portfolio" was Latin America, Haiti was part of my concerns. Since the Clinton administration had a very keen interest in Haiti, I wound up going on a regular basis to meetings of a subcommittee of the National Security Council to coordinate policy and actions as to that country. Since the chairman of my subcommittee was a bit threatically inclined, he scheduled as many meetings as he could in the White House Situation Room. For a native of a small Caribbean island who grew up in a very insular environment, being called for meetings at the White House Situation Room was quite a treat.

One of my memorable anecdotes at the Situation Room involves a conversation I had with one of my counterparts at another government agency. We had developed a very good personal rapport and we chatted about everything when waiting for the meetings to start. He did not particularly like the chairman of our subcommittee (nor did I, but I kept my opinion to myself) and one day, in the Situation Room, he began making rather unflattering comments about him. I told him if he though it wise to make those comments where we were. He responded: "Do you think they are taping us?" I answered: "Do you think they are not?"

Passport by post

Good things come to an end, and sometimes not exactly at the juncture that we plan. Destiny plays tricks on us and we sometimes feel boxed in, when probably we are not. I was caught in a web of assorted difficulties towards the end of my career as a Foreign Service Officer. So my departure from the Foreign Service was rather theatrical.

First, there was the unexplainable difficulties with my landlord concerning the security system of the house we had rented. Now, once you live abroad in countries with a generalized security problem you, naturally, become security conscious. One of the motivations to rent this particular house in suburban Maryland was the fact that it had a security system already installed. Needless to say, being the security system in working order when we rented the property, we expected it to be maintained in working order by the landlord. This was misplaced reliance on my part, to say the least.

One evening we tried to engage the security system and it would not engage. The next day, we called the landlord's agent and we reported the malfunctioning of the security system. Initally, we were told that it would be fixed. Well, the days became weeks and we put our foot down and we told them we would look for another place if they did not fix the problem.

At the same time, my mother-in-law, who had recently become a widow, began having serious health difficulties. A campaign was begun by all my in-laws for my wife and I to return to El Salvador as soon as possible so that my wife would look after the care of my mother-in-law.

Meanwhile, we decided to make good on our threat and we vacated the house with the faulty security system, placed our furniture in storage and moved into temporary housing until we sorted things out. Possibly this sealed the subsequent concatenation of events, but at that time it was seen by me as simply a temporary measure while we sorted out things.

After a couple of weeks in temporary housing it became evident that my wife was not in the mood to look for new housing in the Washington, DC area. My exasperation was such that I decided to cut short my assignment in

Washington by the procedure known as curtailment. I looked for possibilities and I found a position in a Caribbean country where the new American Ambassador-designate, whom I knew personally and with whom I got along exceedingly well, was looking with someone with my background and skills.

Well, things got thicker. My then supervisor was furious when she found out that I was trying to curtail my assignment and move abroad. She told me in so many words that I had betrayed her; that she had given me an opportunity to do economics work in her office, that she needed me there for that extra year (it was a two-year assignment) and that she would try to scuttle my bid to depart ahead of schedule.

My wife was not supportive of any option which would have resulted in my remaining in the Foreign Service. Obviously she thought the quandary I was in was perfect. She did the necessary legwork and found me a job in her country. I felt the noose tighten around my neck.

Then I went to my ophthalmologist for a check up. My ophthalmologist informed me that I could no longer wear contact lenses because I had a condition known as a vascularization of the cornea. My options were to return to regular glasses (very thick ones due to my severe myopia) or had an eye operation to correct my vision. Since I did not want to go back to thick glasses after so many years, I decided to have the operation performed.

Given that I was seeking to go to a very underdeveloped country, I thought it best to have the operation performed before my departure. I figured that I should have no difficulty in securing the necessary medical leave for the operation and recovery so I put in, as a good employee, my application for medical leave with sufficient time and I scheduled the operation.

Meanwhile, my wife had departed the Washington, DC area to be with her mother in El Salvador. So, when the leave denial came back I was home alone in rented furnished quarters.

Problems always come in clusters. While all this is going on, Hurricane Georges strikes my native Puerto Rico and I suddenly loose contact with all my blood relatives. Since the news were of a catastrophic strike to the island, I was very much concerned about the very survival of my relatives.

Home alone, with an eye condition that needed some sort of resolution, with the fate of my relatives unknown, with an unsympathetic surpervisor threatening to do anything in her power to make impossible my curtailment and reassignment abroad, the rope gave way, but not without a final effort to stay the course.

Friday afternoon, all things happen on Fridays in the Foreign Service, I decided to go to the personnel office of the Department of State. They, of course, sided with the supervisor stating that the surgery was elective (which I must admit, technically it was) and that the needs of the service outweighed my personal preference to have it done before my reassignment abroad.

Wanting to exhaust remedies, I then went to the American Foreign Service Association and pleaded with them to intercede. Well, they did, but the results were predictable. Five o'clock came and I left the building thanking everyone for their efforts on my behalf and assuring everyone that I would think things through over the weekend.

I went back to the rented quarters and I tried once more to get through to my relatives in Puerto Rico. I could not get through to anyone in Puerto Rico. I tried calling my wife but I could not get through to her. Lonely and overwhelming was the feeling.

So, the next morning, I turned the keys of the apartment into the rental office, forfeited the rental deposit and took a plane to the city where my surgery was going to be performed the next morning. I had the surgery (which was not 100% satisfactory) and two days after I mailed my diplomatic passport with my resignation to the State Department Personnel Office. So ended my career as a Foreign Service Officer.

Now, there was an effort on the part of the powers that be in the Department of State to keep me in the service. We had a couple of telephone conversations, some of them more supportive than others. However, I felt that I could not go back on my decision decision on account of the determined attitude of my last supervisor at the Bureau of Economic Affairs to do everything within her power to make my career in the Foreign Service as difficult as possible on account of her perception that I betrayed her.

That fear was not unsupported by lore. All Foreign Service Officers have a personnel file and a "corridor reputation." The corridor reputation serves as a sieve before the actual personnel folders are opened to assess the qualifications of the officer for the position he is applying for. Since my last supervisor was a Senior Foreign Service Officer, I knew that she had the access to make sure that I was tagged as a trouble maker.

There is justice after all

My diplomatic life, however, did not end with my departure from the Foreign Service of the United States, much to my surprise and that of many others (undoubtedly for entirely different reasons).

After my departure from the Foreign Service, I resettled in El Salvador, the country of citizenship of my wife. After quite a bit of effort, I was admitted to the practice of law in El Salvador and I set up my own law office.

Having always supported humanitarian efforts by Catholic organizations, it was natural for me to become a Knight of the Sovereign Military Order of Malta when I was invited to become a knight. Since I have always been active in the organizations that I belong to, I was right from the beginning a very active Knight of Malta in El Salvador.

After approximately one year in El Salvador, I was appointed Minister Counselor of the Embassy of the Sovereign Military Order of Malta to the Republic of El Salvador in recognition of my interest in the Order's humanitarian projects in the country. This position, although unpaid, did have all the privileges and immunities associated with accreditation as a diplomat. My appointment was at the request of the ambassador of the Order to El Salvador, who had a hidden agenda of his own for my appointment.

After approximately seven months as Minister Counselor, my predecessor informed that he intended to retire and asked me if I would consider accepting the job of ambassador if it was offered to me. He clarified that the position was, like the one of minister counselor, not remunerated and, in addition, I would have to cover out of my own pocket all office and representational expenses. I did not hesitate one second. Every diplomat's dream is to become one day ambassador and this was being offered to me.

I cautioned him that it would not necessarily be easy sailing getting me appointed to replace him. I reminded him that we both knew that there were plenty of very well connected persons hovering in the background who were ready to jump into the fray to get that appointment. His response to me was: "Let me take care of the politics." And he did.

The year 2000 marked a Holy Year of the Catholic Church. The Order of Malta, in support of the Vatican's initiative, organized a pilgrimage to Rome for knights from around the world. I was strongly urged by my predecessor to participate in the pilgrimage and make myself known to the members of the Sovereign Council who would be making the appointment. There is an old Latin saying, *verbum sapientis satis*.

Following his advice, when I arrived in Rome I telephoned the Chancery of the Order at Via dei Condotti and asked for an appointment to make a courtesy call on the Counselor for Diplomatic Affairs. I saw nothing pushy in this since this was a normal courtesy given that I was then a member of the Order's diplomatic corps. After a suitable interval, I got a telephone call back from the Chancery giving me the date and time for my courtesy call.

When I arrived for the courtesy call, I was greeted by the Counselor for Diplomatic Affairs with the salutation: "Congratulations." When he saw my baffled look he asked: "You have not been told? You are the new Ambassador to El Salvador."

Effective January 1, 2001, I became the Ambassador Extraordinary and Plenipotentiary of the Sovereign Military Order of Malta to the Republic of El Salvador. I held that position until December 30, 2009 when I resigned to return to America, my country. But between those two dates I had a very satisfying time.

San Salvador, March 5, 2001

No. 105

Excellency:

I have the honor to acknowledge receipt of Your Excellency's note dated March 1st, 2001, informing me that on this same date, you have presented to His Excellency The Vice President of the Republic of El Salvador Licenciado Carlos Quintanilla Schmidt, the Letters of Credence appointing you as Ambassador Extraordinary and Plenipotentiary of the Sovereign Order of San Juan of Jerusalem, of Rodas and of Malta in El Salvador.

I would like to take this opportunity to express not only my personal congratulations but also my best wishes for a successful mission. At the same time, I am sure that the excellent relations that exist between our respective diplomatic missions will be maintained.

I avail myself of this opportunity to express to Your Excellency the assurances of my highest and distinguished consideration.

Rose M. Likins

His Excellency

Dr. Juan Manuel Bracete Mari,

Ambassador Extraordinary and Plenipotentiary of

the Sovereign Order of San Juan of Jerusalem, of

Rodas and of Malta,

San Salvador.

LA ORDEN NACIONAL JOSÉ MATÍAS DELGADO
REPÚBLICA DE EL SALVADOR. C.A.

SAN SALVADOR, 25 DE ENERO DE 2010.

SEÑOR EMBAJADOR:

TENGO EL AGRADO DE DIRIGIRME A SU EXCELENCIA, EN OCASIÓN DE COMUNICARLE QUE EL SEÑOR PRESIDENTE DE LA REPÚBLICA, DON MAURICIO FUNES, JEFE SUPREMO DE LA ORDEN NACIONAL "JOSÉ MATÍAS DELGADO", HA TENIDO A BIEN OTORGARLE DICHA ORDEN NACIONAL, EN EL GRADO DE GRAN CRUZ PLACA DE PLATA.

AL EXPRESAR A SU EXCELENCIA, MIS MÁS SINCERAS FELICITACIONES POR TAN MERECIDA DISTINCIÓN, ME VALGO DE LA OPORTUNIDAD PARA REITERARLE EL TESTIMONIO DE MI ALTA Y DISTINGUIDA CONSIDERACIÓN.

EL DIRECTOR GENERAL DE PROTOCOLO
Y ORDENES

EMBAJADOR MANUEL LÓPEZ
SECRETARIO DE LA ORDEN

EXCELENTÍSIMO SEÑOR
DON JUAN MANUEL BRACETE
EMBAJADOR EXTRAORDINARIO Y PLENIPOTENCIARIO
DE LA SOBERANA ORDEN MILITAR Y HOSPITALARIA DE
SAN JUAN DE JERUSALÉN DE RODAS Y DE MALTA.
PRESENTE.

"Brevet notifying conferment of the Grand Cross, Silver Star, of the Jose Matias Delgado National Order for services to the Salvadoran People during tenure as Ambassador of the Sovereign Military Order of Malta to the Republic of El Salvador."

Attempting to influence policy

Being an ambassador gives you access to decision makers. Access to decisions makers is an intoxicating stimulant. Although one does not have the authority to change policy, one does have the opportunity of being heard on a one-to-one basis. This access generates in one the desire to see how far one can go and affect the thinking of those that can change policy. My appointment as Ambassador of the Order of Malta to El Salvador gave me that access and I was smitten by its powerful allure.

The Order of Malta has managed to survive as a sovereign entity by adapting to changing circumstances over the centuries. Originally an organization protecting the Holy Land and later access to the Holy Land through the Mediterranean Sea, with Napoleon's takeover of the island in 1798 on his way to Egypt, the Order developed into a Catholic noblemen's organization to promote humanitarian assistance to those in need.

I took to heart the goals of the Order as its ambassador to El Salvador. I promoted the viability of the Order's health centers for the destitute and I promoted humanitarian assistance in general to charitable organizations in El Salvador. That work on my part legitimized the access that I had to the persons able to formulate, set, change and implement policy in El Salvador.

As an attorney by training, I have always been attracted to legal issues and to the rule of law. During my years in El Salvador, there were a number of issues on the table involving the Salvadoran state's responsibilities under international law. Naturally, I was had more than a passing interest in those issues.

The United States government at the time had two very specific policy priorities involving the rule of law in El Salvador. One of them was the control of criminality in general and the other one, a far more touchy issue to Salvadorans, the extradition to the United States of persons taking refuge in El Salvador to avoid prosecution in the United States. I decided to help, officiously and without consultation, the American embassy in El Salvador in its pursuit of those policy goals. This I did by, what else, writing in the newspapers.

My first article drew on the copious literature in international law concerning the duty of states to preserve law and order within their borders and the responsibility towards other states by damages to foreign nationals caused by the failure to comply with that duty. The lack of response to the article was deafening. I prefer to think that the lack of comment on the article was due to its too learned character. I guess the right answer will be in the government archives.

The second article was counseling the change of the Salvadoran constitution to allow for the extradition of Salvadoran citizens to face prosecution abroad. The Salvadoran constitution, like that of a number of Latin American countries, forbids the government from extraditing its nationals to face prosecution abroad. The United States government had advocated with the various governments of the day changing the constitution to allow for the extradition of Salvadorans to face prosecution in the United States. The efforts had been, and continue to this day to be, unsuccessful.

The article argued the point in term of the promotion of justice and the avoidance of impunity. I thought I had done a very good job of advocacy. Again, there was a deafening silence.

From then onwards, I decided to promote my pet public policy concerns in one-to-one encounters with Salvadoran government officials, members of the diplomatic corps and local opinion leaders.

I now realize that my actual impact on general policy issues in El Salvador as Ambassador of the Order of Malta was very limited. But I do not regret having made the effort nor do I feel that it was a mistake to make the effort.

Influencing policy

The position of Ambassador of the Order or Malta is ad honorem; one does not get paid to do it. Furthermore, one is not given by the Order of Malta an expense allowance or otherwise subsidized for the expenses associated with the position. Therefore, one has to either be independently wealthy or engage in some sort of trade or business to carry on the duties of the office.

Being an accredited ambassador and carrying out a trade or business is tricky. On the one hand, the Vienna Convention on Diplomatic Relations contains a prohibition on engaging in a trade or business;[4] however, it does envision that that may actually happen.[5] In reality, it is not that simple. Among the problems facing a working ambassador, especially one that deals with people and not with things as his trade or business, is that potential clients will always think that they have some sort of advantage by engaging your services. Potential clients have to be disabused of that thinking.

I had a law practice in El Salvador when I was appointed ambassador. I did not close the practice. However, I limited my practice to giving advice and not engaging in negotiations with other parties. Needless to say, this limited my practice considerably. And one does have to make ends meet.

The solution proved to be unique. I became a technical advisor to the Ministry of Public Security and Justice of El Salvador. The position was

---

[4]   ARTICLE 42 of the 1961 Vienna Convention on Diplomatic Relations provides: A diplomatic agent shall not in the receiving State practice for personal profit any professional or commercial activity.

[5]   ARTICLE 31 of the 1961 Vienna Convention on Diplomatic Relations provides: 1. A diplomatic agent shall enjoy immunity from the criminal jurisdiction of the receiving State. He shall also enjoy immunity from its civil and administrative jurisdiction, except in the case of: . . . (c) An action relating to any professional or commercial activity exercised by the diplomatic agent in the receiving State outside his official functions.

tailored to take into account my duties as ambassador while at the same time giving value for the honorarium I was being paid by the Ministry.

Prior to my entry into the Foreign Service of the United States, I had spent approximately seventeen years practicing immigration law in the United States, both within and outside the government. In El Salvador, the Ministry of Public Security and Justice is the ministry in charge of immigration matters. At that time, the new Minister of Public Security and Justice wanted to bring in his own people to the immigration bureau, but those persons did not have technical knowledge of immigration matters. The glove fitted the hand.

The interview to be contracted was an exercise in the utmost tact and mutual deference. The Minister did not want to discuss remuneration, although he had an amount in mind. He needed my advice, but he knew that I could not commit full time to the ministry. So, the initial contact was in the nature of a social call, focusing on the needs of the ministry and leaving aside any mention of how I would satisfy those needs.

The actual details were discussed with an intermediary who was a good friend of both of us. Essentially, my remuneration would amount to approximately one half of the salary of the Director General of Migration, but I only had to commit to the equivalent of 4 hours per day, the hours and days being of my choosing from day to day. The arrangement satisfied all of us.

The first issue of wide ranging implications that I had to give advice on was the implementation of the regional visa coordination treaty. This treaty, like many other treaties nowadays, was a framework for arriving at decisions from time to time binding on all parties. The problem was that the specific decisions were not to be made by foreign affairs specialists, but by immigration specialists, who were not necessarily knowledgeable of the niceties of treaty law. And, of course, problems developed as to how to interpret the various accords that were reached from time to time.

The Ministry of Foreign Affairs of El Salvador eventually got involved in the discrepancies as to the interpretation of the treaty and the accords reached under the treaty. Their interpretation did not coincide with the provisions of the law of treaties, now basically, although not entirely, codified in the 1969 Vienna Convention on the Law of Treaties. Foreign Affairs and Public Security pretty much came head to head.

I was called upon to give my advice on the interpretation and enforcement of the various documents agreed upon by the directors of immigration of the Central American countries that had signed the treaty. My initial brief memorandum got lengthier and lengthier as it was further modified to take into account the objections and arguments of the Ministry of Foreign Affairs of El Salvador. My interpretation on the validity and precedence of the various documents eventually was accepted as the correct one. My research eventually got published as a law review article.[6]

Immigration policy is closely linked to foreign policy generally. Sometimes immigration policy does affect the internal politics of the country. That was one of the challenges faced by the Minister of Public Security and Justice with the nationals of a certain Latin American country that was very much interested in the outcome of the 2009 elections in El Salvador

Under the working accords reached under the Treaty for the Creation of the Sole Central American visa, the nationals of that country were exempt by all signatory countries from the requirement to secure a visa prior to entry into the country. Consequently, the government of El Salvador at the time was in the dark as to who was coming to El Salvador from that country until they actually made it to the port of entry. That was deemed unacceptable due to the suspicion that a large number of individuals entering as tourists were in fact government agents coming into the country to lend assistance to the opposition party (that eventually won the elections).

The Minister of Public Security and Justice thought he had his hands tied. The Ministry of Foreign Affairs could not offer any alternative to the situation. I was asked to provide a legal justification to impose visas on the nationals of that country that would acknowledge the working agreements under the Central American treaty.

Well, I figured one of the basic principles of international law is reciprocity. The government of the country involved required visas of nationals of El Salvador, regardless of purpose of entry. I offered the Minister the reasoning that in light of the overriding principle of reciprocity, that visas would be required of nationals of that country notwithstanding the Central American agreement to exempt them from visas. The Minister signed off on the recommendation and it was notified to the affected country and to the signatories of the Treaty for the Creation of the Sole Central American Visa. No country objected to the decision taken by El Salvador.

My third policy success dealt with the El Salvador's responsibilities to control precursor chemicals for the production of methamphetamine. The national entity with responsibility for El Salvador's antinarcotics efforts was within the Ministry of Public Security and Justice. El Salvador had been notified on more than occasional that it was in arrears in the passage of legislation to control precursor chemicals.

In a conversation with the Minister, this issue was discussed and he indicated that he had been unable to have the Legislative Assembly of El Salvador approve the required legislation to control precursor chemicals.

---

[6] "Ad Hoc Treaties: The Sequel to the Treaty for the Creation of the Sole Central American Visa," Vol. 24, No. 1 Internat. L. Q. 8 (Summer/Fall 2008).

Of particular importance at that time was pseudoephedrine that was freely available in El Salvador with no control whatsoever. There were rumors of entire shipments being sold and exported to neighboring countries with tighter regulations.

In conversations with acquaintances with medical knowledge, it surfaced that many substances were being controlled administratively by the Ministry of Health of El Salvador through the framework of the control of lethal agents by forbidding the sale without a prescription of a substance in an amount equal or greater than the minimum lethal dose. Pseudoephedrine, in a sufficiently large amount, can be a lethal agent.

Armed with this knowledge, I requested an appointment with the Minister of Health of El Salvador, and presented him with the problem being faced by the Minister of Public Security and Justice that he had not been able to secure passage of legislation to control pseudoephedrine. I asked him if he would be willing to invoke his authority under the control of lethal agents to regulate the sale of pseudoephedrine pending the approval of appropriate legislation. He made one phone call and the issue was placed on the agenda of the next meeting of the board with authority to do so. I earned my honorarium for that day.

MINISTERIO
DE SEGURIDAD
PUBLICA Y JUSTICIA
Construyendo la Paz Social

Ministro

May 28, 2009

Dr. Juan Manuel Bracete
Calle Tecana No. 26
Antiguo Cuscatlán
El Salvador

Dear Dr. Bracete:

A the end of your tenure as a valued member of my team at the Ministry of Public Security and Justice, I would like to express my gratitude for your efforts in assisting this Ministry in the following matters which resulted in solving difficult problems faced by us and that appeared intractable at the time.

I would like to congratulate you for your brilliant research and guidance on the matter of the implementation of the Treaty for the Creation of the Sole Central American Visa and the manuals provided under the treaty. Your analysis of the applicable principles of public international law was instrumental in deciding how to proceed at a moment when we had differences with other government agencies on the subject matter.

Thanks are also due to you for your well reasoned analysis of the constraints and flexibility in the application of the Treaty for the Creation of the Sole Central American Treaty when we were faced with the need to impose more restrictive entry requirements for Venezuelan nationals. Your guidance was instrumental in convincing other agencies that we could, indeed, impose those more restrictive requirements without violating our treaty obligations.

Your insight in finding the legal basis for the control of pseudo-ephedrine pending legislative action, and your invaluable intervention with the Ministry of Public Health of El Salvador, allowed us to comply with various bilateral and multilateral agreements that engage El Salvador to control the movement and sale of that chemical.

Lastly, I would like to thank your intervention that resulted in the removal of hazardous chemicals left behind by a dependency of the Ministry of Public Works of El Salvador when that dependency transferred to the General Directorate of Migration and Alienage certain real estate. Your timely and resourceful intervention resulted in the removal of the chemicals and the threat of action by the environmental authorities against certain of the functionaries of that General Directorate.

Wishing you the best in your future professional endeavors, I remain

Rene Mario Figueroa Figueroa
Minister of Public Security and Justice

Life after being abroad

My return to the United States after spending five years nine months in the Foreign Service and eleven years in Central America was much smoother than what many people thought it would be for me. After all, I came back as a private citizen after having been in close contact with people at the highest levels abroad and being deferred to in many situations. The transition for some is very difficult.

I have always adapted to circumstances. I have never thought anything I had was an entitlement. I knew and know that you get back in proportion to what you put in. The more effort, the more reward. Sometimes that reward is simply emotional.

I enjoy the anonymity of the large American cities. It is such a relief to be able to walk in shorts and tennis shoes without caring who sees you. It is also a relief to be able to have a drink with friends and express your opinions without having to edit your speech for the sake of your role. Although I am not retired and I still work as an attorney, I have a lot less stress than during those years abroad.

Security is also an issue when you have been abroad. American citizens abroad, except in very few countries, are obvious targets. Being able to walk down the street without having to scan your surroundings for possible threats is one of the great joys of being back in your country. That has no price. It is great to be back home.